AN OUTLI
OF THE HIST
OF THE CATH
BURMESE MIS

Volume the
f i r s t
concerning
B u r m a
issued in
the Series
Bibliotheca
Orientalis
published
by the
W h i t e
O r c h i d
P r e s s
Bangkok
Anno 1996

AN OUTLINE OF

THE HISTORY OF THE CATHOLIC BURMESE MISSION

FROM THE YEAR 1720 TO 1887

Paul Ambroise Bigandet

Originally Published in Rangoon in 1887

Paul Ambroise Bigandet
AN OUTLINE OF THE HISTORY OF
THE CATHOLIC BURMESE MISSION
First published: 1887
Reprinted: 1996

Published by
WHITE ORCHID PRESS
98/13 Soi Apha Phirom, Ratchada Road,
Chatuchak, Bangkok 10900 Thailand.
Tel. (662) 930-0149 Fax. (662) 930-5646

Printed in Thailand
Publication supported by
an Open Society Institute project

BIBLIOTHECA ORIENTALIS
is a reprint series of studies and research
monographs concerning Asian subjects

La BIBLIOTHECA ORIENTALIS
comprend une série de réimpressions
d'études et de recherches sur l'Asie

ISBN: 974-8299-75-9

AN OUTLINE

OF THE

HISTORY OF THE CATHOLIC BURMESE MISSION

From the Year 1720 to 1887.

COMPILED BY THE HEAD OF THE MISSION.

RANGOON:
PRINTED AT THE HANTHAWADDY PRESS.
1887.

AN OUTLINE OF THE

HISTORY OF THE BURMESE MISSION

FROM ITS BEGINNING

IN THE YEAR 1723 DOWN TO THE YEAR 1863.

DOCUMENTS respecting the beginning and progress of the Pegu and Ava Mission, having, owing to several adverse circumstances, completely disappeared, the writer has been reduced to the sad position of an humble gleaner collecting, with much trouble and labour, a few particulars, that will enable him to give an imperfect sketch and a faint outline of the history of this Mission.

The Barnabite Fathers who have during a century cultivated with much zeal, talent and labour this portion of the good man's Vineyard have much written on Burma, its language, population, religion and literature. The writer has seen a catalogue of the several works composed by the above mentioned erudite Fathers, and left behind them chiefly for the benefit of the missionaries newly arriving from Europe, who in a short time, and with ease, could appropriate to themselves the fruits of the experience and labours of their predecessors. His impression derived from the perusal of this catalogue may be assimilated to the emotion a merchant feels in perusing a bill of freight after he has lost his vessel. A considerable part of these writings had been stored up in the Church of Khiansarua as in a perfectly secure place, when the building was totally destroyed by fire, in 1840, during the absence of the Rev. Father N. Polignani then engaged in erecting the Missionary's house at Monhla. With the view of keeping some order in the disquisition of the subject under consideration, and enabling the reader to obtain the information he wishes to gain on the various localities where missions have been established in former times, or are still existing in our days, it is intended to follow the subsequent plan.

1st. We will endeavour to ascertain from what quarter came originally the Christians we find, up to this day, established in Upper Burmah, in the Capital and in Villages, situated north and west of the Capital.

2nd. We will detail at length the establishment of the mission, under the auspices of the Barnabite Fathers and its continuation for a while, by a few Priests, sent to Burmah by the Council of the Propaganda. We will likewise give a brief account of the mission, under the administration of the Fathers Oblats of the B. V. and relate the transaction whereby the said mission was made over to the Missionaries of the French Seminary of the Missions Etrangeres.

3rd. Finally, we will sketch out a short outline of the various stations, and localities where up to this day, Christian congregations are still existing.

This little labour can scarcely be considered as a matter of choice, but of absolute necessity to rescue from oblivion facts of the highest interest to this mission—facts which would be soon buried into absolute oblivion. The old missionaries that are the living witnesses of many of them, are but few, and will soon have disappeared, carrying into the tomb what they have learned from their predecessors and also what they have seen in their own days.

ORIGIN OF THE FIRST CHRISTIANS WHO WERE LOCATED IN UPPER BURMA.

Origin of the Upper Country Christians.

The Christians that were found in several localities West of Ava by the first Barnabite Missionaries in the beginning of the last century, descended from a certain number of Europeans and Eurasians, whom the chance of war threw into the hands of the victorious Birmans. The latter, according to a long established custom, took their prisoners to their capital, and treated them with great kindness. Fearing, however that the bold foreigners, were they kept all together in the Capital, might organize a plot against Government, or support the cause of some pretender to the crown, the reigning monarch adopted towards his captive foreigners a line of policy that exhibited the fear he had of their courage and resolution. He had them scattered over the distant provinces of Shoaybo, Tabaring and Ahlong, that is to say, in the tract of land between the rivers Mu and Khyindouin. There they lived in peace, without trouble or molestation in the same localities where up to this day we meet with their descendants.

Place the Christians at first occupied.

That the first Christians in Burmah were not natives converted to Christianity, but foreigners chiefly Europeans, and native Christians from the Coromandel and Malabar Coasts, there cannot be the slightest doubt. We have in support of this assertion the very name given to the Christians by the Burmese as indicative of the foreign origin of the former. They are always called *kalas* or Western foreigners. Their religion is mentioned as the religion of the foreigners. To distinguish them from the Musulmans who are also called *kalas*, our Christians are often named *phringies* or *feringies* which appellation was imported into Burmah by Mussulmans from India. Judson in his dictionary erroneously translates the word *phringie* by Portuguese. It is merely the name given to all Christians by the inhabitants of Western Asia. From them, those of Central Asia and India have received it. There is no doubt that it is the name Franki slightly corrupted, which, from the days of the Crusades, has been used all over Asia by the Mussulmans to indicate the Christians in general. During the campaign in Afghanistan, the English were called *feringhis* by the natives of that country.

Origin of the Christians.

They are named Phringies.

The opinion of the Burmese on this point is so strongly adhered to, that they still give the name of *kala* to such descendants of Christians, who have apostatized and live, labor, and in many instances, worship as the Burmese. They look upon them as people of a distinct origin, and in no way belonging to their race. When speaking of these apostates, they join the word *piet* to that of *kalas*, indicating that they are lost, spoiled, etc., but the epithet of *kalas* remains fastened on them.

The first Christians that appeared in Burmah in the beginning of the 17th century, were certainly foreigners. In a short time they assumed the dress of the people among whom they were living, became cultivators of the soil and with the exception of religion and fellowship in worship, they were in everything assimilated to the natives of the soil.

They dress and work like the Burmese.

The few natives that became converts, joined with the Christians, and being merged into the community were called *kalas*, because in the opinion of the Burmese, they had embraced the religion of the Kalas and had become *bonâfide* strangers, having lost their own nationality. This is a strange and somewhat startling fact, but the writer has had numberless opportunities of ascertaining the true opinion of the natives on this point. How often he has heard a Burman speaking of one of his countrymen, willing to become a Christian, "he wishes to become a *kala*." Indeed, with the people of these parts, religion and nationality are so intimately connected, so thoroughly blended together, that they form one and the same whole. Religion cannot be forsaken without giving up nationality, and in other words, the fact of embracing the religion of another people, is equivalent to becoming a member of the same social or political body.

WHENCE CAME THOSE CHRISTIAN FOREIGNERS WHOM THE FIRST MISSIONARIES MET IN UPPER BURMA.

This is a question that has never been satisfactorily answered. The archives of the mission having been completely lost, recourse must have been had to the meagre accounts to be found in the collection of Voyages, and also in the manuscripts and printed works of the bold adventurers that visited this country during the 15th, 16th and 17th centuries. The first Europeans who appeared in these parts, were Merchants who after having travelled through western Asia, Persia and India, came to Pegu. These worthy lovers of lucre, seem, from their accounts, to have been animated with a praiseworthy curiosity, and impelled with a strong desire to know new countries, and become acquainted

Whence came the first Christians.

with the populations and productions of the land they visited. Some of them having won the confidence of the rulers of these countries, have had opportunities of becoming acquainted with some political transactions and have left to us the only records we possess of events that have taken place in these distant lands. To their praise let it be added, that most of them, agreeably to their humble abilities, kept a regular journal wherein they consigned the results of their observations. These journals were eagerly sought for and perused on their return, by their countrymen, amongst whom a thirst for knowledge had been awakened and quickened by the spirit of discovery that prevailed chiefly in southern Europe during the the 15th Century. It cannot be denied that many of these travelling merchants have been often led into error either by the information they received, or by a want of accurate observation, but notwithstanding these defects inseparable from the exceptional position of these men, who had no time to make themselves acquainted with the language and habits of the inhabitants of the countries they visited, their records are the only sources left to us to come to a superficial and imperfect knowledge of the state of these countries, two or three centuries ago. To them only we are indebted for the means of answering the question above referred to.

The Kingdom of Pegu.

In the latter part of the 16th Century, the Kingdom of Pegu had reached the highest point of greatness and extent. The Ruler of that country had subjected to his arms, part of Arracan Burmah and overran with his victorious army, the Shan States as far as Zimmay. He was the most powerful sovereign of the Peninsula beyond the Ganges. But this prosperous position of affairs lasted a very short time. Under the reign of the son of the greatest King Pegu ever had, calamities of the worst description befell in succession, the ill fated Kingdom. The Kings of Arracan and Tounghoo joined their arms and vigorously attacked the Peguans. Their efforts were crowned with a complete victory.

Agreeably to the custom of these half civilized nations in their wars, they destroyed everything that they met with, sparing neither men nor animals, neither private dwellings nor places of worship. From the testimony of father Bowes a jesuit Missionary who happened to be in that country in 1600, it appears that the whole country was covered with ruins and the carcasses of men and beasts. The good father says that the river was so covered with masses or heaps of dead bodies, half burnt planks and timber of every description, that it was with great difficulty the ships sailing up the river could force there way through them.

Philippe de Britto settles at Syriam.

The confederates were indebted for their great success to the valuable assistance they derived from a body of adventurous Portuguese, under the command of Philippe de Britto. The King of Arracan who had engaged them in his service, offered them, in full property, the port and town of Syriam. De Britto eagerly accepted the proffered gift, and took immediate possession of the place with his followers. It is probable that he occupied it in the name and for the benefit of the Crown of Portugal. Two or three years after, de Britto, with a view to strengthen his position and probably with the intention of giving a greater extent to his little state and become the founder of a considerable Settlement, went over to Goa to explain personally the state of affairs in Pegu and ask for some reinforcements. Nothing is positively known respecting the result of his application, but it is not unlikely that the Portuguese Viceroy would let pass such an excellent opportunity of obtaining a strong and permanent footing in a country famous for its fertility and in particular for the great quantity of gold and precious stones it yielded. Be that as it may, certain it is that de Britto came back attended, at least, with a number of followers. To his great surprise he found himself, on his return proclaimed King of Pegu by his adherents.

His doings

From that time de Britto carried everything with a high hand. His manners became haughty and he had the impudence, nay the ungratefulness to offer repeated offences to his friend and protector, the King of Arracan. He tried to give some stability to his situation by marrying one of his sons named Simon, to one of the daughters of the King of Martaban. It is probable that de Britto in his proceedings, gave to the King of Ava, many reasons of complaint. In the spirit of a true adventurer, that knew not to set bounds to his ambition, he thought he had no precautions to take with a barbarian King living far in the interior. But he soon found out his mistake, and paid dearly for his haughty behaviour and insolent proceedings.

His miserable end.

In 1614 the King of Ava, elated with the extensive acquisition of territory which the disasters of the Peguans had given him a fair opportunity to make to his dominions, came down the Irrawaddy with a powerful armament, and beseiged Syriam. For a long time, the Portuguese retaining as yet the bold and daring spirit of the conquerors of India, made a desperate resistance and baffled the efforts of the enemy. At last, de Britto was betrayed by the natives at his service, into the hands of the Burmese who put him to death, after having cruelly tortured him.

The Burmese led captives into their country the prisoners made at Syriam.

On this occasion, the Burmese King inaugurated a line of policy which has been subsequently followed by his successors under similar circumstances. Proud and self-conceited, as the Burmese are, they could not help acknowledging the superiority of the Europeans over them in many things of great concern. After having reeked their vengeance on the unfortunate chief of Syriam, the Burmese spared his companions and followers and led them captives to Ava. Among them was the wife of de Britto, whose name has been preserved. She was called Dona Maria de Saldanha. The number of these foreigners living in the same place gave some uneasiness to the Burmese Government. A certain number of the ablest among the captives were kept at Ava, and had for business to teach the Burmese what they knew about military matters. As the Burmese scarcely knew anything respecting gunnery, the Christians of the capital were intrusted with the management of the Artillery, and up to this day, they have remained the chief gunners or Artillery men in Burmah. The other Christians were removed in the distant provinces of Tabaring and Ahlong between the rivers Khyin-douin and Mu. As will be hereafter noticed, they settled in villages. They were exempt from the payment of tribute, but they had to bear the weight of the Military service, in the same way as they do now.

Their position under Burmese Government.

In this little sketch borrowed from the narratives of old travellers, we find the true and unmistakeable origin of the christian congregations that were then, and are now existing in the Upper Country. To corroborate this statement and to place it beyond the possibility of a doubt, we have a tradition to be met with in all Christian villages. During his pastoral visit in 1861, the writer questioned the old and best informed men of the villages, respecting the epoch their ancestors had arrived in this country. They all gave him the year 999 of the Burmese Era, as the epoch when this event happened. There would be a difference of 33 years between the year 1614, when Syriam was conquered by the Burmese, and the year 999 above-mentioned. But the reckoning of the later period may begin at the time when de Britto made his appearance in these parts and in that case the difference or discrepancy would become so small as to be almost insignificant. We may consider it, as a well-established fact that the first quarter of the 17th Century is the true period of the beginning of those Christian congregations which are now found in Upper Burmah, and that those foreigners were Portuguese. By the word Portuguese we must understand not only the Europeans of that nation, but likewise, *mestesos* or those born of the union of Europeans with native women, who at that time must have already formed a numerous class. Moreover, there must have been amongst the followers and supporters of de Britto, a good number of Negroes and pure natives, from the Malabar-Coast that had embraced the Christian religion.

Probable epoch of their arrival at Ava.

The son of the conqueror of the Peguans, following up the career of conquests opened by his father, steered his victorious course in a Southern direction and possessed himself of Tavoy. Thence he went down by the sea to the mouth of the river Tenasserim, with the intention of making himself master of the flourishing city of that name, situated on the southern bank of that river at the very place, when after having from its source, followed a Southern direction, bends on a sudden, and shapes its course towards the West. Here he was met by Christopher Rebello, Portuguese Commander who with two well-equipped vessels, attacked dispersed and partly destroyed the Burmese fleet composed of

Defeat of the Burmese fleet at the mouth of the river Tenasserim.

more than 500 boats. This blow saved the city of Tenasserim and stemmed the tide of conquests in that direction. This reverse did not prevent the Burmese Sovereign to follow up his conquest in the south-easterly direction, towards the Shan State of Zimmay, under the pretext that it had formerly belonged to the Peguan Monarchs. His success was complete. A little time previous to the above-mentioned event, the chief of the English factory established at Siam, had despatched in 1716, a certain Thomas Samuel, to Zimmay, then a place of considerable importance, with the purpose of establishing commercial relations. Samuel had scarcely resided there for sometime, when the King of Ava took the city, carried to Ava, with Thomas Samuel, his attendants, and the several foreigners, Dutch and French, that were residing in that place. On this occasion, the number of Christian foreigners in the upper country was a little increased by the arrival of the European captives brought from Zimmay. It seems, from certain papers found in the archives of Fort St. George, Madras, that European traders had established factories at Syriam, Prome, Ava, and as far as the then town of Bhamo during the course of the 17th Century. In the latter place, situated at a distance of five or six miles from the present Bhamo, in a northern direction, are to be seen the ruins of a considerable brick building which was pointed out to the writer as having been the place were foreigners lived and had their godowns or store-houses. What became of those factories and of the people in charge of them, it is probable that, agreeably to the custom of the Burmese, many of these merchants were induced to stay in the country or were detained by force, when the Burmese Government could find a pretext for resorting to such harsh measures. The Dutch, the English and the Portuguese appear to have traded with Ava during the abovementioned Century. The foreigners must have been numerous at Ava in 1658, the year when a large Chinese army invaded Burma and beseiged Ava. We know that the Artillery of the place was served by them. Indeed it was to their skilful management of that arm, that the Burmese were indebted for the safety of their capital and the repulse of the invaders.

Success of the Burmese in the Shan States.

During the early part of the 18th century, no event seems to have

Short lived success of the Peguans in about 1740.

happened calculated to influence other foreigners to come and settle in the country. A little before the middle of the 18th century, the Peguans had, at first, successfully shaken off the fear they had of the Burmese. Emboldened by the miserable condition in which that State had fallen, they advanced as far as Ava, made themselves masters of the capital and of its Sovereign, and indeed of the whole country. They however remained but a few years in possession of the new conquests. A bold adventurer of the Province now called Shoay Bo, known afterwards under the name of Aloung Pyah, gathered a few resolute men, attacked and drove away the small garrisons the Peguans entertained in the Provinces, West of the Irrawaddy.

Defeated by Aloung Pyah.

His small number soon swelled into a large and powerful army. He crossed the Irrawaddy, laid seige to Ava and took it after an obstinate resistance. Pursuing the flying Peguans, he invaded their own territories, and appeared with his victorious army before Syriam, the principal seaport of Pegu, and the centre of a considerable and active trade. The resistance was long and obstinate. During the seige, Aloung Pyah seized a small French vessel loaded with arms and provisions for the Peguans, which had unfortunately got aground in the river. In a fit of rage, the Burmese King ordered the Captain of the vessel to be put to death, but took into his service all the people found on board. Syriam having, at last, from want of provisions, been obliged to surrender, Aloung Pyah carried away into his dominions all the foreigners found in the place.

Taking of Syriam.

Foreigners carried to Ava.

Finally, under the reign of Tsinphioo Shyin, the second son of Aloung Pyah, the kingdom of Siam was successfully invaded by the Burmese. Juthia, then the capital of that kingdom, was taken by storm. The conquerors carried back with them the Vicar Apostolic and a portion of his flock. The Prelate was subsequently allowed to proceed to Pondicherry. As to the Christians most of them were removed to Ava. The writer has seen in 1856

Taking of Juthia by the Burmese.

two very old men who were brought over from Siam, among the captives.

Conclusion from the above related particulars.

From all what has been just stated, we may infer the following conclusions :—1st, the arrival of the Christians in the upper country of Burma dates from the middle of the first-quarter of the 17th Century. Those Christians were chiefly Portuguese and Natives of Western India. 2nd, the number of the first comers received at different successive periods, an accession of foreigners belonging to different nations. 3rd, the taking of Syriam by Aloung Pyah in the middle of the last century brought a fresh increase of foreign Christians, chiefly French and Dutch. 4th, the Christians of Upper Burma are principally the descendants of Europeans, carried into that country during the various periods above stated. 5th, the natives that embraced Christian religion have amalgamated with the descendants of the foreign Christians, and by intermarriage have produced the mixed race that dwells in the Christian villages now existing.

It is a remarkable fact that despite the great effect that must have been produced by the accession of the predominating Burmese element, the Christians of Burma exhibit unmistakable signs of their primitive origin in the features of the face. They have all without exception, lost their family names, which would at once reveal the origin of their ancestors, but on a close examination of their personal appearance, particularly of the face, we can, with perfect ease, trace up their origin. At Monhla, for instance, the writer remarked an old man with green eyes, and a face of the Dutch type. With other people, the French features could not be mistaken, whilst with most of the people dwelling in the village of *Khiaonio*, an observer could not fail to remark the striking resemblance between them and the descendants of the Portuguese, such as we see them, on the Western coast of the Indian peninsula and in the Straits of Malacca.

2.—THE MISSION UNDER THE BARNABITE FATHERS.

No record previous to 1722.

No records exist at present in Burma, on the state and condition of the Mission previous to the arrival of the Barnabite Fathers in the year 1721. At that time, we know that there were two Portuguese priests, one at Syriam and the other at Ava. The former was in charge of the mixed Christian populations composed of foreigners, who for the purpose of trade, lived in the sea-port. The other attended to the spiritual wants of the Christians dwelling in the capital. Those priests were sent over from Meliapor to Burma by the Bishop of that place. In all likelihood they were Goanese priests, or Christian natives of the western coast of India raised to the priesthood.

Goanese Priests.

These ministers of Religion were not zealous for propagating the saving truths of the Gospel among the Gentiles. Indeed, they were similar in their manners, habits and capacity to those of the same caste whom we meet with now in different parts of India. They never cared for the conversion of the Gentiles. They limited their efforts to the discharge of the sacred ministry's functions, among the Christians; nor did they ever take the trouble of learning the language of the country. They spoke the Portuguese language, or rather a certain patois having some affinity with that language. It is probable that from the capital they went into the country for the purpose of visiting the Christian villages, and ministering to the spiritual wants of the people. It is owing to those occasional visits, that we are indebted for the preservation of the few congregations that still remain. Had they been left to themselves without the presence of a priest, it is probable that faith would soon have become totally extinct, and the smallest vestige of Christianity would have for ever disappeared. Indeed, owing to the scarcity of those pastoral visits, many small communities of Christians have gradually become apostate. They have not embraced paganism, though they follow many of its practices, in deference to the Burmese. They are indeed without religion, and in many instances the members of the communities that have apostatized, are the worst characters in the country. They are called by the Burmese *Kalapiet*, or apostates. We will hereafter devote some remarks upon the subject of these unfortunate people.

Arrival of the Barnabite Calchi.

In 1719, the Holy See had sent Monsignor Mezzabarba with a great retinue, as an ambassador to the Emperor of China, for the purpose of disposing that Ruler to treat with kindness the Christians of his empire, and allow them liberty to practise and preach the Gospel through his dominions. Among those who accompanied the prelate, there were five fathers of the Barnabite order. The mission having met with little or no result in China, the ambassador sent two or three of the Barnabites to Cochin-China, kept one with him, and sent the fifth named Sigismond Calchi to the Pegu Mission, in company with another priest of the name of Joseph Vittoni. Monsignor Mezzabarba, who was Pontifical Legate, gave to Calchi all necessary powers and jurisdiction over the places he was sent to.

He comes from Macao.

Persecuted by the Goanese priests.

The new Missionaries were badly received by the Portuguese priests, who went so far as to lay snares for their destruction. But Providence saved them from those many dangers. The best among the Christians soon discovered the difference between the newly arrived Missionaries and their own priests. They admired the sterling merits of those two apostles, and protected them from the machinations of their enemies. They had been represented to the King of Ava as spies, who had come from China with the secret intention of supplying his enemies with particulars that might prove detrimental to his interests. The best and most influencial among the Christians, pleaded on behalf of the innocent Missionaries with so much success, that the King despised the slanderers and showed the greatest kindness to the worthy priests. He then sent back Vittoni to Europe, with presents for the Holy Father. Meanwhile he gave to S. Calchi the permission to circulate freely throughout his dominions, and preach the Christian religion. His mortified life, his zeal in sowing the good seed, weakened his constitution. He fell dangerously ill. The hatred of the Portuguese priest had reached such a pitch of inveterate hatred, that he refused to come and administer to the holy man, the last rites of the Church. But, fortunately Providence managed things so admirably, that George Rosetty, priest of the Propaganda, arrived a few days before his death, and had time to console the apostle, and comfort him with the Holy Sacraments. Calchi saintly died in Ava at the age of 43 years, 1728. He had composed a small dictionary for facilitating to his Brethren that would succeed him, the study of the Burmese language.

Death of Calchi.

Two months after, another Barnabite father, named Gallizia, arrived at Ava. After a short stay in the capital, he came to Syriam, built a church, and laboured with an admirable zeal for the conversion of the Gentiles, and the spread of Christianity. Seeing that alone he could do little, and that the little good that would be effected, would, after his death, vanish away, he resolved to return to Europe, represent the position of this mission to the superiors of his order, and to the S. congregation. Having put his design into execution, he obtained in Italy all that he wanted to place the mission on a strong and lasting basis.

Arrival of Father Gallizia.

He was consecrated Bishop of Elisma *inpartibus*, and returned to the mission with Paolo Nerini, Alexandro Mondelli, John del Conte, and a lay brother, Angelo Capello, an able physician. They all left Italy in 1741, embarked at Lorient in France and arrived at Syriam in 1743.

He returns with five Fathers.

On their arrival, they found that the Peguans had revolted and shaken off the yoke of the Burmese, and were making themselves masters of their capital. It was impossible to think of proceeding to Ava on account of the war raging between the Peguans and the Burmese. They all, with the exception of P. Nerini, went to the royal city of Pegu. They were well received by the King, who gave them permission to preach the Gospel, and granted them a piece of land for building a church.

An unforseen occurrence soon happened, which put a stop to the progress of the rising mission, and placed it in the worst possible position. A squadron of six ships, commanded by the Chevalier of Sconenville, Governor of Banky bazaar,(Serampore)a Danish factory,

Unfortunate arrival of a powerful Danish squadron.

Transaction of the Dutch Admiral.

appeared before Syriam. Bishop Gallizia who then was in that place, was deputed by the Peguan Governor, to the commander of the squadron, to ascertain what his views could be. The latter stated that the factory of Banky bazaar having been ruined by the peoples of the neighbouring country, he was coming with the intention of seizing on Syriam, making it a European factory, and restoring the power of the King of Ava in Pegu. The Bishop remonstrated with him, pointing out the injustice of seizing upon a country which did not belong to him. At last the commander was prevailed upon to visit the Peguan Governor, and come with him to some understanding. It was agreed upon, that the admiral would proceed to Pegu with a certain number of soldiers and officers.

His voyage to Pegu town.

The Bishop was ordered to accompany the party and act as interpreter. They arrived safe to the Royal city, and were received with signs of an apparent friendship. The King, it was said, being in the country, it was necessary to wait for his return, before any arrangement could be made. The treacherous Peguans thought only to gain time in order to compass more effectually the ruin of the strangers. The Bishop having been informed of what was going on, gave immediate communication of it to the admiral. It was agreed that

He is massacred with his officers the Bishop and three priests.

they would leave instantly the place, and withdraw to their ships. They were no sooner embarked than they were attacked by swarms of enemies from both banks of the stream. At that moment, the water in the river was very shallow. They came to the determination of leaving the boats, and returning by land to Syriam. This resolution was the cause of their ruin. They were all killed in the jungles, with the exception of four men, who escaped and went to give a timely warning to their companions who remained in the ships. The Bishop, who had fled with them in company with the Admiral and his men, was involved in the common ruin with Fathers Mondelli and de Conte.

Before giving a sketch of the fatal contingency that ensued from this lamentable event, we must mention one fact relating to Syriam which is not known generally, but which had almost revived the Mission at that place.

In the year 1744, during the war between the Peguans and the Burmese, a body of 10,000 men of the latter fell on a sudden, on Syriam, took the place, and destroyed, as is usual with them, all that came in hand. This success was of short duration. The Peguans rallied, and with the large reinforcements that poured in from all directions, attacked, defeated and almost exterminated all the invaders. This victory of the Peguans proved almost as fatal to Syriam, as the invasion itself. Indeed, the Peguans seemed to be bent on completing the destruction of that unfortunate city. The Mission's buildings were consumed by fire, with the exception of the church which, however, was robbed of all its furniture.

Political transactions.

Let us resume the course of events. The sad and overwhelming news of the death of the Bishop and of his two companions, had not yet reached Father Nerini, who was at Syriam with brother Angelo. He had however received several letters making him acquainted with the critical situation of the Europeans in the capital. He wisely withdrew from Syriam with brother Angelo and concealed himself in some parts of the country. It was in the place of his concealment, that he heard for the first time of all the particulars of the catastrophe that had befallen the Bishop and his brother Missionaries. He at once provided for the safety of brother Angelo, by sending him out of the country, on board of a ship. A little while after, seeing the impossibility of doing anything for the benefit of his flock, without exposing himself to certain death, Nerini wisely determined to leave the country. He went by sea to Mergui, then a Siamese seaport. After a stay of eight months at that place, he crossed the Bay of Bengal, went successively to Pondicherry and Madras. In the latter place he met with brother Angelo. Both went to Chandernagore, with the hope of finding a ship bound to Syriam. After a lapse of some months, they embarked on board of an English ship bound to Syriam, and safely reached that place in April 1749. On his arrival, the Missionary was greeted with enthusiasm not only by his flock, but likewise by all the foreigners residing in that city. They offered him all the assistance he needed for repairing the evil lately done to the mission.

Critical position of father Nerini at Syriam.

He leaves the country.

He returns to Syriam.

With the assistance of a very worthy Armenian named Nicholas de Aguilar, and of his wife Margaret, he erected a fine brick church, 80 French feet in length, 31 in breadth and 30 in height, to the vault. That part of the building was never finished, on account of the delay that occurred in procuring workmen from the Coromandel coast, and the war with the Burmese that soon followed. The church had but one nave, and was adorned with columns and arches both inside and outside. There was on the western side a turning stair-case, screw like, whereby they ascended on to the top of the building. When the church was finished, the same pious benefactors gave to the zealous priest, the means for building a large house for the residence of the Bishop and priests he expected from Italy, and also for accommodating a good number of students. Adjoining to the church, and in a vast enclosure, he erected a large house for the reception of young orphan girls. In gratitude for his benefactors, Nerini had the following inscription, engraved on a marble slab, placed in the church.

Builds a brick Church.

D. O. M. ad fidem Propagandam, Clerici Regulares Sancti Pauli, Nicolao de Aguilar, Natione Armenus, Magarita Conjux Ædificabant, Anno Domini 1750.

The zealous servant of God laboured earnestly for the promotion of Catholic religion, not only amongst Pagans, but also amidst the Armenians who were very numerous and wealthy in that emporium of trade. In the year 1753, he reconciled to the Church the Armenian priest and had the following inscription placed on his grave, in the new Church.

Convertion of an Armenian priest.

Hic jacet Petrus Joannes, filius Asphami, Natione Armenus, religione Sacerdos, qui in Sinu Eccl. Catholicæ, Moriens Anno Domini 1753, ætatis suae 61, pracclarum religionis examplum suis imitadum reliquit.

The active and zealous Nerini, in the midst of his apostolical labors, found time to revise and perfect a Grammar and Dictionary of the Burmese language and composed a catechism and prayer book. Whilst engaged in these occupations, he received the distressing news of the loss of four fathers of his congregation, two of whom perished in

His literary labors.

the Gulf of Mártaban almost in the sight of the shores of Pegu. In the same wreck, were lost the letters of the sacred Congregation, appointing him Bishop and Vicar Apostolic. It was in 1756 that this sad occurrence happened. But this misfortune, great as it was, did not dishearten in the least, this incomparable servant of God, He went on with his missionary labors, with the same zeal and fervor though a cruel war was raging at that time between the Burmese and Peguans. The former, under the leadership of Aloung Pyah, having driven away the Peguans from Ava, pursued them down all along the Irrawaddy, until they reached Syriam, which they immediately invested.

Burmans beseige and take Syriam.

The conqueror set fire to the suburbs, and occupied the church and Mission's buildings. During that time Brother Angelo, when engaged in assisting and curing the wounded, was killed by a cannon ball. A small French vessel appeared before Syriam, with warlike stores for the Peguans. The commander not well acquainted with the river, anchored at high water in a place which proved to be a sand bank with but two feet of water at ebb tide. It fell a prey to the Burmese. Aloung Pyah suspecting that Nerini had perhaps solicited this assistance from Pondicherry, gave, in a fit of passion, orders to behead the innocent Missionary, and bring his head to him. The soldiers charged with the execution of this barbarous order knew and appreciated the virtues of the good priest. They killed a Portuguese priest and carried his head to Aloung Pyah. The monarch soon perceived that this was not the head of the devoted victim. He sent them back with positive orders to bring to him the head of the European priest. This time the orders were too faithfully complied with. This melancholy event occurred in the beginning of the year 1756.

Death of Father Nerini.

Building of Rangoon. Two new Priests from Europe.

In the year 1760 arrived at Rangoon, the new city built by Aloung Pyah, at a small distance from Syriam, on the easternmost Branch of the Irrawaddy, two Barnabite Fathers Sebastian Donati, and Pio Gallizia, a nephew of the former Bishop who was involved in the same ruin with the Danes who had proceeded to Pegu.

The former, after a stay of but a year in the mission, died at Ava, probably in the village of Khiaong-oo. Gallizia proceeded from Rangoon to Ava. In the year 1761, two new fathers arrived from Europe to the Mission, Avenati and Percotto. Nearly four years after this timely arrival, the Mission had to meet with fresh misfortune. Gallizia died of dropsy at Shoay Bo then the capital. His bones were subsequently removed to the village of Khiaong Oo, and a few months afterwards, father Avenati died at Rangoon. In this manner, Percoto found himself alone in the mission during the period of 5 years. It was but in the year 1767 that he had the happiness to see four new Missionaries arrive in this portion of the Vineyard which he had cultivated alone during many years. They were Gerhard Cortenovis, Melchior Carpani, Antonio Re, and Ambrosio Miconi, (the latter died in the village of Kioun dau). A little while after the arrival of these fellow labourers, father Percoto had to come to Rangoon for some affairs of the Missions. There he received the apostolical bull and the letter of the S. Congregation informing him of his elevation to the episcopal dignity, with the powers of Vicar apostolic. But the great difficulty was to find a consecrator bishop. Whilst deliberating with much perplexity, about the place he had to go to, in order to receive the episcopal consecration, there arrived at Rangoon, in the beginning of the year 1768 Mgr. Brigot ,bishop of Tabraca, Vicar Apostolic of Siam, who had come over from Siam, with the Christian captives, after the taking of Juthia, by the Burmese, under their King Tsin bioo Shiin. Father Percoto was consecrated with the title of Bishop of Maxula. He composed, with the assistance of a learned Burmese, an extremely well written book of controversy in the shape of a dialogue between a Christian and a Burman. In the year 1772, two new labourers arrived in the Mission from Europe. These were Marcel Cortenovis and Caejetan Montegazza. It appears that the Bishop of Meliapoor continued to claim spiritual jurisdiction over the Burmese Mission, because we find him complaining bitterly of the conssecration, of Mgr. Percoto having been made without his consent or approbation. But his complaint was groundless, since the S. Congregation in the letter, addressed to the Bishop elect, had distinctly stated that he

Percoto elected Bishop.

Arrival of two new labourers.

could receive the episcopal consecration from any Bishop he might chance more easily and conveniently to meet in any part. Another fact no less worthy of remark that, that there had always been at Rangoon Portuguese priests sent from Meliapoor to minister to the spiritual wants of that part of the congregation which called themselves Portuguese. These Priests resided in a suburb of the city called Tat galay, nearly south-east from the present Jail. They had a small church to which was attached the Priests dwelling. These unworthy ministers nourished in their hearts a deadly animosity towards the excellent and zealous Barnabites, whose apostolic life was a perpetual censure of their disorderly conduct. We have already noticed the infamous behaviour of those unworthy priests towards the first Barnabite Missionaries that came to Burmah. After a lapse of nearly fifty years, their rancor had not abated. In the year 1773 after having in vain twice attempted to poison the worthy father Carpani, the Portuguese Priest had the boldness to go, attended with a few followers, and stab him with his own hands within his own compound. The knife fortunately being wielded by a weak and perhaps trembling hand, was entangled in the folds of the victim's dress, and inflicted but a slight wound. The neighbours attracted by the noise, rushed to their pastor's assistance and saved him from a certain death. The murderer was arrested. Being a priest and a foreigner, it was agreed that he would be sent to his ecclesiastical superior in Madras, and dealt with according to the law. He was put on board of a French ship bound to Madras. The vessel ready for sail, was anchored at the mouth of the Pegu river. At the ebb tide, the infamous Priest asked leave to bathe in the river, in a place, where there was little water. He was no sooner in the stream than an enormous alligator seized him by the waist, and after having kept him for a while above water in the sight of the crew, disappeared with its prey in the depth of the river.

Misbehavior of a Portuguese priest at Rangoon.

When this lamentable occurrence took place in Rangoon, the Vicar Apostolic was at Monhla, busy in promoting the cause of religion and establishing a seminary for the education of young natives, destined to become Catechists and valuable auxiliaries of the Missionaries. He was assisted in the foundation of that Institution by two students of the College of the Siamese Mission, left to him by Mgr. Brigot. As soon as he heard of these disturbances, the Chief Pastor hastened to Rangoon to restore order, and do away with the scandal which so many infamous deeds had occasioned. Meanwhile he came to the resolution of sending Father Carpani to Rome for the purpose of giving to the sacred Congregation, an accurate statement of the Mission, and also to obtain its approbation of the various Burmese works he had composed, and if possible, to have them printed at the Propaganda Press Father Carpani was also instructed, to call at Meliapoor, on his way to Europe, and make the Bishop of that See acquainted with the infamous behaviour of the priests of the Burmese Mission who were under his jurisdiction. After a stay of seven years in Rangoon, Father Carpani took his departure in the year 1764. He was succeeded by Father Gerard Cortenovis. Having thus arranged the affairs of the Mission at Rangoon, the Bishop returned to Ava. His time was devoted in fulfilling the duties of a zealous pastor and in writing books in the Burmese language and above all in the composition of a dictionary in Burmese, Latin and Portuguese.

Providential presence of Bishop Brigot at Rangoon.

Father Carpani sent to Europe.

Death of Bishop Percoto.

His constitution, naturally not very strong, was still weakened by his incessant labors, and above all by his very poor diet. During the latter part of the year 1776 he grew daily weaker and at last died at Ava in the arms of his friend, the chevalier Millard, at the age of 47 years. He was assisted in his last moments by Father Montegazza who had hastened from Nabeck to Ava on hearing of the dangerous state of his superior. Bishop Percotto spent only 14 or 15 years of his life in the Mission. He was a man of remarkable attainments and his abilities were of a superior order. He had become thoroughly acquainted with the Burmese language. The writings in that language which he has left behind him, are monuments of his uncommon proficiency in Burmese. Unfortunately for his successors in the same field, many of his writings are now no longer extant. The dictionary that had cost him so much labor, the translation of Genesis and of the Epistles of St. Paul, are lost. There remain the larger Catechism, the controversy between a Christian and a Pagañ and the Gospels and Epistles for Sundays and festival days throughout the year. We have also in poetry an abridgement of the book of Genesis, the book of Tobias and that of Daniel. The book of Tobias was translated by Mgr. Percoto, but it was subsequently written in verse with Genesis and Daniel, under the care and supervision of Father Joseph D'Amatto.

Father Cortenovis nominated Vicar Apostolic.

He died on his return from Madras on of the Nicobars.

Father Gerard Cortenovis was appointed to the charge of Vicar Apostolic. He went to Meliapoor in 1779 when he received the episcopal consecration with the title of Bishop of Sozzopolis. He took his passage to return to his Mission, on board a vessel that touched at the Nicobars on her way to Rangoon. During the stay of the ship in those islands, the new Bishop died. This sad event took place in 1780.

Father Lewis Grondono-Josi D'Amato arrived from Europe.

It was a few years previous to this, that the celebrated Father Lewis Grondono arrived in the Mission. It appears that it was in 1777 or 1778. He had to pass through an ordeal of severe trials and long sufferings before he reached the port of Rangoon. He was wrecked on or near the Island of Madagascar. He was subsequently rescued from that miserable place, with twenty of his surviving companions, by a Dutch ship which took them to the Cape of Good Hope. From that port the zealous Missionary found his way to the place of his destination.

Father Montegazza proceedto Europe.

He is followed by a Burman named Tsau.

What induced Father Montegazza to proceed to Europe, since Father Carpani had already been deputed thither by Mgr. Percoto, to make known the wants of the Mission. We have no reason to account for the taking of such an important step except the sudden and unexpected death of the Bishop of Sozzopolis, and perhaps that of Father Carpani himself. Be that as it may, certain it is that he returned to Europe in 1784, taking with him two Burmans, one of whom named Tsau, was an ex-Talapoin. This man had become a fervent convert. He wrote a very elegant account of his voyage, in Burmese. Some parts of this work are still extant in the hands of one Christian of Upper Burmah. Assisted by the learned ex-Talapoin, Montegazza had printed at Rome, in Burmese characters, in 1786, an alphabet, a small Prayer Book, and a Catechism, with the Latin translation. After the completion of this undertaking, Montegazza was consecrated Bishop of Maximianopolis, and in the following year, returned to the seat of his labors, with two fellow labourers, named Butiromonti and Azimonti.

He had some books printed at Rome in Burmese.

The superior of the Barnabite Order seems to have had greatly at heart the advancement of the Burmese Mission. At the instances of Father Carpani, he had sent out Father Louis Grondono, and Father Roverizio. The latter appears to have reached his destination in 1781. Two years after, Father Sangermano and Joseph Amato left Italy and arrived at Rangoon in the month of July 1783.

Father San Germano and Josi arrived in Burma in 1721 and 1793.

All these new Missionaries went to the Upper Missson, with the exception of Father Sangermano who remained at Rangoon with Father Marcel Cortenovis. These worthy Missionaries were most of them, men of great learning and eminently fitted for the duties of accomplished Missionaries. But owing, it seems, to the little care they paid to their diet and also to unnecessary exposure, many died after a very short stay in the Mission. Thus Roverizio having been scarcely two years in the Mission departed this life in 1783 at Khiaong Oo. Butiromonti had not been more than a year in the village of Khiansarua, since his arrival in Burma when he died in that place in 1788. His tomb is to be seen in the cemetery of that village. Azimonti had, by the oraers of Mgr. Montegazza, proceeded to Mergui, the southern boundary of the Burmese dominions. He had scarcely been there during a few months when he was seized with a violent fever. Hoping that a change of place might prove conducive to the restoration of his health, he embarked on board of a vessel, bound to Pondicherry. The anchor had just been dropped in the roadsteads of that town, when he expired.

Death of three Barnabites Fathers.

Father Joseph D'Amato was stationed at Monhla where he resided during the greatest part of his long Apostolic career. Father Lewis Grondono was often residing at Nabek. To them, devolved the entire care of the congregations spread in the various villages. Mgr. Montegazza had his head quarters in the new Capital Amarapoora, founded in 1786 by the king known as Bodophra. He too, came to his end, in that city in 1794. His tomb with a suitable inscription is in the Christian cemetery of that Capital.

Fath. Joseph D'Amato.

Death of Bishop Montegazza.

At the end of the last century, and in the beginning of this, Rangoon carried on a most flourishing trade. Its port was resorted to by a great number of ships, of various nations. These favorable circumstances attracted to that mart of trade, a great number of foreigners. The number of Christians, both natives and strangers, amounted to nearly three thousand. At that time there were two churches at Rangoon, one of which, in the town, was built of timber, agreeably to the custom of the Burmese. Adjoining to it, there was an orphanage that served as a school for the girls, and also an asylum for the maintenance of children of that sex, who were left destitute and unprovided for.

The church was known under the title of "Assumption." Father Marcel Cortenovis remained in charge of it until his death, which happened in 1802.

Death of Cortenovis.

The other church, that of St. John the Baptist, was built of brick, with walls and pillars of strong masonry. The position occupied by that sacred building is well known. It extended in a northerly direction, from the verandah of the Sister's Convent, known now as St. John's Instutition. The writer saw, in 1856, small brick pillars, which had served to support the verandah in front. For it was surrounded with a verandah, designed to protect the building against the rain, and afford a sufficient space for a procession. Here was stationed Father Sangermano. To that church was connected a school, under his able direction, which was frequented by no less than 60 or 70 boys.

From that school have come out two young native priests, Fathers Ignatius de Britto and John Koo, as well as several men who have subsequently followed various professions. Both churches were destroyed by the Burmese, when the English appeared before Rangoon, with their fleet, in 1824.

Sangermano goes to Rome.

Sangermano, since the death of so many missionaries, and particularly that of his companion, Marcel Cortinovis, had often written to Rome, and to his superiors, to solicit the aid of new laborers. But owing to the invasion of Italy by the French armies, and the seizure by them, of all monastic properties, and also to the deadly war between France and England, he was for many years without receiving any reply. At last he resolved to make a voyage to Europe, to try to obtain, by his personal solicitations, what had hitherto been denied to his applications by letters. He stationed at Rangoon, Father John Koo, who had been, not long ago, elevated to the priesthood, and left for Europe in 1806.

His voyage lasted nearly two years, and he reached his country in 1808. During his stay in Italy, he published a very interesting work on the Burmese Empire, which has since been translated into English. Sangermano saw his position beset with great difficulties. Neither his Congregation, which was dispersed, nor the sacred Congregation, which was left without resources, would afford him the aid he had gone to solicit. After a stay of ten years in Europe, Sangermano thought to return to his mission. He had gone to Leghorn to secure his passage on board of a vessel bound to India, when he was seized with a disease that carried him off in a few days, in 1819.

Father Grondono.

When Sangermano went to Europe, there remained but two European priests in the mission, Fathers Grondono and Amato, and two natives. Of the latter, Father Koo died a little while after Sangermano's departure. This casualty compelled Father de Britto to come to Rangoon, and minister to the spiritual wants of the Christian community of that place.

College at Nabek.

For some reasons, which it would be too long to detail in this short outline, the college founded at Monhla by Bishop Percotto, had been removed to Nabek, a village finely situated on the western bank of the Irrawaddy, a little above the place where the great river Khyndouin discharges its waters into that mighty stream. He could not

4

have much time to bestow on the institution, since he had to take care of the Christians in the capital, and of those living in the village of Khiaungoo.

From what has been reported to the writer, by many old men who knew him, and had been his disciples, Father Grondono was a man of very superior attainments, and well versed in the natural sciences. The father of the present King held him in the highest respect, and always mentioned his name with veneration. He had been heard to say that there had never been before, nor will there be afterwards, a man like Father Don Lewis. He lived to an old age, and died at Amarapoora in the year 1822. His virtues and his talents were so much admired by the first men in the court, that, contrary to an almost invariable custom of the Burmese, an order was issued allowing his mortal remains to be interred in the precincts of the church.

Death of Lewis Grondono at Amarapoora.

Father D'Amato, himself very old, remained alone in charge of the several congregations of Upper Burma. Despite his age and infirmities, he visited yearly the different stations, and finally died at Monhla in 1832, after a stay of 49 years in the mission. He had received a very superior education, and was an accomplished Burmese scholar. He knew well the Pali language. He has left behind him a collection of sermons and pious instructions, written in a very superior style. He had made a collection of plants, and executed drawings of the insects and reptiles of Upper Burma. He gave to the English Resident, Col. Burney, a part of his drawings and collections. The remainder must have perished with all the manuscripts of the mission, in the conflagration that destroyed the church and priests' house at Khiansarua in 1840. He was the last of the Barnabite fathers, who had been in charge of the Burmese mission, during 112 years. During the eventful war of 1824 and 1825, Father D'Amato was left free and undisturbed, whilst all the Europeans, not excepting even Father D'Britto, were arrested, loaded with irons, and kept in close confinement with imminent danger to their lives, until the conclusion of the war, that is to say, during nearly two years.

Death of Jose D'Amato.

Death of Fath. DeBritto.

Father De Britto, since he took spiritual charge of the Rangoon Church, resided always in that city until his death, which took place in 1836.

We have to a certain extent anticipated the course of events in order to bring to a conclusion the few particulars we have gathered here and there, with much trouble, respecting the Barnabite Fathers who must be considered as the real founders of this mission. They have been preceded in this field by the Portuguese priests, sent from Meliapoor, by the bishop who claimed jurisdiction over Pegu and Ava, but they contented themselves with the care of the Christians residing both at Syriam and Ava. They never troubled themselves about the spread of Christianity among the heathen. They would not even condescend to learn the language of the natives. They spoke Portuguese, preached in that language, and made it the distinctive characteristic of Christians. From what we can gather here and there, some of the priests continued to remain in the Mission, until the beginning of this century, at least in Rangoon. But it does not appear that they occupied the Ava stations, long after the Barnabite Fathers' arrival. They lived at Rangoon in a quarter of the suburbs, called Tatgalay, a little south west of the residence of the Chief Commissioner, Colonel Phayre.

We have now to trace back our steps and come to the time when the Sacred Congregation thought of sending assistance to the Burmese mission, which for several years, was taken care of, by only two Priests, father D'Amato in the Upper Country, and father DeBritto, at Rangoon.

Reasons of the fathers of the Burnabite Order giving up the Burmese Mission.

The Order of the Barnabites had previous to the epoch of the French Revolution, made the greatest efforts to keep up the mission confided to the care of their society. They had dispatched at various times, the very best men of their illustrious body But the wars that desolated Pegu and Burmah, the difficulties to keep up stations in those troubled times, the insalubrity of the climate in several parts of the country ; the want of a proper diet, particularly for the new comers in the country, the austere mode of life many of the missionaries led with more zeal than discretion ; all these causes contributed to thin the ranks of the devoted propagators of the Christian religion, and to bring to an untimely end, a good number of them. These losses weakened much the Order at home, which had received already several blows during the occupation of Italy by the French, that is to say until the downfall of Napoleon in 1815. The heads of the Society resolved to give up the Burmese Mission. To that effect they supplicated the Sacred Congregation to have it confided to some other religious body.

THE MISSION UNDER THE PRIESTS OF THE PROPAGANDA, AND THE OBLATS OF THE B. V. M.

The Mission made over to Priests of the Propaganda.

The Sacred Congregation having been made aware of the intentions of the superior general of the Burnabites Order, and at the same time, being apprised of the sad situation of the Burmese Mission caused by the absolute penury of missionaries, lost no time, in selecting labourers to cultivate that portion of the Vineyard. In 1829, they appointed the Revd. Frederick Cao, as head of the Mission. He was consecrated Bishop in the beginning of the following year, at Rome. In that city, he was joined by the Rev. Domingo Tarolly, a secular priest, and a Tyrolese by birth, and also by the Rev. Antonio Rica, a Genoese. They left the eternal city in the same year, took their passage on board of a ship bound to Alexandria; thence crossed the Isthmus of Suez; embarked again on board of a small Arabian craft bound to Jedda. In that place they were fortunate enough to find an English vessel bound direct to Rangoon. Having embarked on board of that ship, they safely came to anchor at Rangoon, about the end of the year 1830.

Bishop Cao.

Father D. Tarolly and Rica.

Father Rica returns to Genoa.

Bishop Cao on his arrival, sent up into Burmah proper his two companions. Father Rica remained at Ava then the seat of Government, and occasionally visited the small congregations, located in the villages of Nabek and Khiaungoo.

His stay in the country did not last long. He was attacked with a serious complaint, brought upon himself by an excessive use of cold baths, during the hot season. He returned to his native city, Genoa, after having remained but two years in the mission. Father Domingo Tarolly hastened to the village of Monhla where he met the venerable father Burnabite Jose D'Amato, the only survivor of so many zealous laborers belonging to the same religious family. From Monhla he went to Khiansarua, where he ministered to the spiritual wants of the Christians living in that and the neighbouring places. The good Jose D'Amato died in 1832, after a stay of 49 years in the mission. Father Tarolly was then alone in charge of the northern portion of the Burmese Mission. It was during this period that the new town of Maulmain together with the surrounding villages including Amherst, at the mouth of the Salween, was detached from the Siamese Mission and made over to the Vicar Apostolic of Ava and Pegu. This measure had been provoked by the representations of Dr. Cao to the sacred Congregation. The alleged motive was that Maulmain being a flourishing place, belonging to the English, it afforded a safe and secure asylum to the members of the Burmese Mission, in case persecution should compel them to withdraw momentarily from Burmese territory.

Maulmain made over to the Burmese Mission.

Father Ignatius Stork.

In the year 1835, the Rev. Ignatius Stork and the Rev. Froidevaux, were directed by the superior of the Propaganda Mission at Macao, to proceed to the Burmese Mission. On their way, from that city, the vessel they had embarked on board at Penang, was wrecked on an island of the Nicobar group, and father Froidevaux was drowned. His companion contrived to save himself, and reached Rangoon, on board of a native craft. Father Stork was sent to the upper country, where he laboured with a great zeal, for several years. Subsequently he was removed to Maulmain, where he remained until the end of the year 1843. He then left the Burmese Mission, and joined that of Bengal. Chittagong has been the seat of his labors for many years. His delicate health obliged him to make a voyage to Europe. Think-

His companion wrecked at the Nicobar.

ing that he had been much benefited by the change of climate, he came back to India, and died, I believe, in Ceylon, on his way to Calcutta.

A Spanish Priest, whose name the writer has not been able to ascertain, came also to this mission in 1836. But he died at Ava, one month after his arrival. Two Priests, on their way to this mission, from Rome, died both, on the same day, from a pestilential contagion at Mocha in the Red Sea. In consequence of so many disastrous occurences, the mission was reduced to a sad condition, owing to the want of labourers.

Two Italian Priests died on their way to the Mission.

Bishop Cao goes to Europe.

Bishop Cao resolved to proceed to Europe for the purpose of obtaining without delay, a fresh supply of missionaries. He left Maulmain, where he was residing in the year 1839. His stay in Europe was of more than a year or two. He came back as far as Calcutta, with two Missionaries. On his arrival at that place, he found a letter of the Sacred Congregation, whereby he was forbidden to proceed farther, and commanded to return to Italy. The order was complied with. He went back to Italy, obtained a small bishopric in the States of the Church, and died in or about the year 1853.

Fath. Boccacio and Bartelli.

The two Priests who accompanied Bishop Cao, from Europe, were the Rev. Boccacio and Francis Bartelli. The former remained in Maulmain but four years, and left the mission in 1843. He went to Bengal joined that mission and subsequently that of Patna, where he is still living. Father Bartelli was sent to the upper country. He was stationed in the village of Nabek, and at the same time had charge of that of Khiaungoo. He was afterwards removed to Maulmain, and placed in charge of a small congregation about a mile distant from the principal church of that town, in a district called Mayangon. He remained in that place, until the end of his life, in the beginning of the year 1856. Father Francis was a man remarkable for his energy and activity. He had studied Burmese with considerable success, and could write with great facility in that language. He has left several pamphlets in Burmese. He carried on for nearly one year, a fierce warfare, or rather a controversy with the Baptist Missionaries of Maulmain, in which it seems he had the advantage. But it is much to be regretted that both parties, in the heat of dispute, would have occasionally allowed passion to supersede sober reason.

Though the mission had not been actually made over to the Society of the Oblats of Turin, one of their members, the Rev. Joseph Enrici, offered his services to the Sacred Congregation, for the Burmese Mission. The cardinal Prefect acceded to his demand, and in 1539, he arrived in Burmah. He was directed to go to the upper country and was stationed in the village of Monhla. He was a man full of zeal and of an ardent temper; but his constitution being somewhat weak, he soon sunk under the influence of an insalubrious climate, and died in that locality after a stay of a little more than a year. He was known under the name of Jose *galé*, or the younger Jose. His tomb is close to that of the last Barnabite father, J. D'Amato, who, is remembered by the native Christians as Jose *gyee*, or the elder José.

The Missions made over to the Oblats of Turin.

It was during the course of the year 1840 that the mission was formally made over to the Society of the Oblats. Whilst the preliminaries for this important transaction were going on between the superior of that society, and the cardinal Prefect of the S. Congregation, two oblats priests left Turin during that year, the Rev. Paul Abbona and the Rev. Vicenti Bruno. They came over through Egypt, called at Aden, touched at the different parts of the Malabar Coast, made some stay in the neighbourhood of Cape Comorin, and at last reached Madras. Thence they took their passage on board of a ship bound to Rangoon and landed safely in Pegu, in the beginning of the year 1846. The Rev. V. Bruno laboured successively in Rangoon and Maulmain. Owing to a chronic dysentry that weakened greatly his strong constitution, he returned to Europe in or about the year 1844, and came back the following year. He remained in the misson until August 1866. Being afflicted with deafness, and having to settle some family affairs, he went a second time to Italy, with the intention of never returning to Burmah. After a stay of about three years in his native country, he, however, altered his

Arrival of fathers Abbona and Bruno.

mind and left Italy again for the East. Being incapacitated by his deafness for the arduous duties of a missionary life in Burmah, he wisely resolved to remain in Calcutta, in the capacity of assistant Priest in the Cathedral church of that city. Up to this moment, he is occupying that situation.

Doings of father Abbona.

The Rev. P. Abbona was directed to proceed to Upper Burmah, and assume charge of the Christian Congregation of Amarapoora then the Capital of that kingdom. He has always resided in that city. In 1856, he went to Europe, and the following year returned to occupy the same situation at Mandalay the new capital of Burmah. He greatly exerted himself in promoting the cause of religion at Amarapoora. Owing to his zeal, a good brick house was built which was subsequently enlarged for the purpose of having a school. He was greatly assisted in carrying on these works by Mr. Antony Camaratta, the principal Christian in the Royal city. During the war of 1852 which secured the throne to the present sovereign to the detriment of his Brother, the then reigning king, Amarapoora was sacked and burnt by the soldiers of the Pretender. Father Abbona had the mortification to see his house forcibly entered by marauding parties of soldiers, thirsting after plunder, who carried away everything, sparing not even the sacerdotal ornaments, which were either destroyed, or profaned by some villains in the midst of the laughter and applauses of their companions. All the other missionaries who had been brought from different parts of the country, in chains, like criminals, solely because they were Europeans, stayed in the mission house, and were exposed to all sorts of indignities from the part of a lawless soldiery. But father Abbona, being the Priest of the locality was repeatedly threatened to be killed, unless he discovered the place, wherein pretended treasures had been concealed. By his coolness and courage, he overawed the marauders, and after the present king had possessed himself of the capital, he was allowed to live in peace, and labor for restoring to its primitive condition, the mission house and the Church. Both had escaped the general conflagration, owing to their being made of solid masonry. In the beginning of 1857, the reigning Sovereign, under the influence of some superstitious notions, hammered into his head by the *Pounhas* or Brahmins, attached to his court, resolved to remove the seat of his kingdom to a place, about six miles north of Amarapoora, called Mandalay, from the name of a small hill lying North East from the new capital. Father Abbona had to remove thither with all the Christians. He had then to build a house and place for worship. As he was held in great esteem by the king, he was enabled to obtain a fine site for himself and his congregation. With aid received from the king and other benevolent persons, he settled himself as well as he could, without imposing any sacrifice on the mission fund, which, at that time, was completely exhausted.

Whilst the two Priests above mentioned were on their way to Burmah, the Superior of the Society of the Oblats formally accepted the Pegu and Ava mission, and took immediate steps for sending reinforcements of evangelical laborers to Burmah. He selected the Rev. Faustino Ceretti as the fittest person to be placed at the head of the mission. His talents, his admirable zeal made him truly worthy of filling up the important situation he was appointed to. He was consecrated Bishop at Rome, in 1842, and soon took his departure with five Priests—Messrs. Delprino, J. B. Pacchiotti, F. Andreino, A. Giotto, and M. Bucalla. There were also two deacons, Messrs. J. Pogolotti, and V. Gabutti, besides five lay Brothers viz., J. Alasia, Francisco, D. Tessio, Benedicte and Moricio. Mgr. Ceretti being rather advanced in years, had the greatest difficulty in learning the Burmese language, which in fact, he could never speak. He applied himself to the study of English, and though he could never speak it fluently, he acquired a very good knowledge of it which even enabled him to keep up a written controversy with the American Baptist missionaries in Maulmain. During his stay of five years in the mission, Mgr. Ceretti never enjoyed good health. He was always in a state of suffering and bodily distemper. Despite such a sad condition, he laboured incessantly with his pen, and often spent a great portion of sleepless nights in reading and writing. As a vigilant pastor, he visited the various congregations of Upper Burmah, endeavouring by his words and example to promote the cause of religion. When he was in the village of Monhla, Mgr.

Arrival of father Ceretti and many Priests.

Doings of father Ceretti.

Ceretti established a school in which, besides the Burmese, the Latin and I believe the Italian languages were taught. Many children belonging to Christian, Burmese and Mussulman families resorted to the school in the beginning, but a few months afterwards, the boys to the number of nearly 70, left the Institution and never returned. After this failure, the good Bishop thought of opening another school in the village of Nabek, in a fine position on the western bank of the Irrawaddy, a little above the mouth of the Khyindouin. A good building was erected for that purpose, but owing to some changes that occurred, the project was never carried into execution. The Bishop entertained many plans, but not one of them has ever been realized. Indeed he was a man of no ordinary parts, his talents were of a superior order, his virtues elicited the admiration of those who knew him, his zeal was active and energetic. Notwithstanding these great accomplishments he failed in most of his undertakings, because he lacked experience which can never be gained but after a long stay in this country. He laboured under two great disadvantages, he knew not the language of the country and he had no one among his fellow labourers, who had influence enough to advise and guide him. Harrassed with bodily sufferings, and mental anxieties, stung to the quick by disappointments which he never anticipated, he suddenly, when in Maulmain, came

Returns to Italy.

to the resolution of leaving the mission. He went back to his native country in 1847, and withdrew in the mother house of his Congregation, where he had what he most valued and cherished, a quiet and retired life, devoting

His Death.

his time to study and prayer, until his death which happened in the year 1854 or 1855.

The Rev. Delprino, soon after his arrival to the mission, was

Rev. Delprino.

appointed Pro-vicar Apostolic and resided in Maulmain, being in charge of the mission in Pegu, during the absence of Bishop Ceretti in Ava. He laboured

Erection of Maulmain Convent.

with great energy to acquire a knowledge of the English language which was the more necessary, as there was, at that time, a full European Regiment and two batteries of European Artillery stationed at Maulmain.

It was in the middle of the year 1843, that the building intended for a convent was begun; but it was completed only during the course of the following year. Father Delprino laboured with great activity for completing the edifice, sparing no fatigue, and exposing himself to the intense heat of a burning sun. It is probable that owing to such excessively imprudent exertions, that his constitution, apparently very strong, was materially impaired. The chest became affected, and the distemper growing worse, his physician advised a change of climate. The patient went over to Madras, and after a stay of three months in that city, he sunk under the complaint and died in the end of 1847.

He died at Madras.

The Rev. Pacchiotti acquired a good knowledge of Burmese and English. He was remarkable for the ardour of his zeal. He has been employed for some time in Maulmain, in Rangoon, in the village of Nabek and latterly was stationed at Thayetmyo. The prints of his zeal are, up to this day, visible in the different places where he has discharged the duties of his sacred ministry. He is fondly remembered by those whom he has instructed in the knowledge of religion. His health being very bad, he was compelled much against his will, to leave the seat of his missionary labors, and return to his native country in 1857. There, he is still living with a much shattered constitution.

Rev. Pacchiotti.

Returns to Europe.

The Rev. Ferdinand Andreino has always been employed in the upper mission, sometimes in the villages of Nabek and Khiaungoo sometimes at Monhla. Now he labors with much zeal in the large village of Khiansarua, having succeeded the very Rev. Polignani in the end of 1859.

The Rev. Giotto remained only two years in the mission. Being always ill, he returned to Italy where he died almost immediately after his arrival. Father Buxala after a stay of four years, spent chiefly in Moulmain and Rangoon, returned to Europe. He reached Malta, but what became of him subsequently, no one has ever been able to tell. He has never been heard of since, in spite of the exertions made, in different countries, by the Sardinian ministers to find him out.

Jacobo Pogolotti after his ordination, laboured for two years in the upper country and afterwards in Moulmain. He was subsequently sent to Bassein to assist the Rev. D. Tarolly, in carrying on the Karen mission. He was a most promising young clergyman; his abilities were more than common and his zeal rather more ardent than discreet. He went to establish himself in the jungle among Karens and conformed entirely to their mode of life. Being a man of a strong constitution he withstood the ordeal for some time, but soon after he was attacked by the jungle fever. Having neglected to take remedy in proper time, he was removed, when too late, to Bassein, and expired in the arms of his fellow labourers, in the year 1849.

Rev. Pogolotti.

V. Gabutti was ordained priest together with the Rev. Pogolotti in the city of Amarapoora by Bishop Ceretti. This unusual ceremony attracted a great number of people, and among others was the Prince of Prome. The Rev. father remained for sometime in the upper country. He came subsequently to Pegu and Tenasserim. For some years, he was stationed at Bassein, and in 1857 he was placed in charge of the congregation of Mayangon, in Maulmain. In 1858 he was removed to Rangoon, where he has labored for four years. In the year 1862, suffering of an ulcer in the mouth, he returned to Italy and died in the following year at Turin. Of the four lay Brothers who accompanied Bishop Ceretti, Brother Francisco died at Maulmain, Brothers Benedict, and Mauricio returned to Europe. The latter has entered the Trappist Order and is apparently in Algeria. Brother Dominico Tesso was ordained Priest in 1861, and is now labouring in the village of Khiaungoo. Finally brother J. Alasia being old, and sick has returned to Europe, in the course of 1863.

Rev. Gabutti.

When Bishop Ceretti had arrived in Burma, some correspondence took place between the Superior of the Oblats on one part, and the Bishop of Madras on the other, for establishing a small community of the Oblats in the Madras Mission. The object of this step was to have in that Mission a body of Priests always ready to labour in ordinary times, in some parts of the Madras Mission, as Missionaries, and also, when required, they would have to preach spiritual

Retreats, either in behalf of some Christian congregations, or for the benefit of the local clergy. These Priests were to live together, forming a sort of community under the observance of the Rules of their Order. Such a plan having been hastily contrived, and hurriedly carried into execution, soon gave unmistakeable signs of a complete failure. In the year 1844 the following Priests landed at Madras. J. B. Balma, H. Gottio and D. Gaffo, with the Brothers Romano, Pasqual and Peter. They remained but a short time in the Madras Mission. Some misunderstanding with the Vicar Apostolic arose, and after a stay of about 18 months, they embarked for the Burmese Mission in the year 1846. The Rev. J. B. Balma was stationed in Moulmain. At the departure of Bishop Ceretti for Europe, he was appointed superior of the Mission. In the year 1848, he was consecrated Bishop of Ptolemais, in *partibus infidelium*. Immediately after his consecration, Bishop Balma visited all the stations of upper Burmah, and returned to Moulmain, where he fixed his residence. By his exertions, the Convent School, under the management of the Sisters of St. Joseph of the Apparition, flourished and had a good number of pupils. The boys' school placed under the able management of Mr. E. Abrew, kept up a high character, and the attendants were very numerous. Unfortunately D. Balma fell sick of the dysentry and was compelled by the physician's advice to proceed to Italy in the beginning of the year 1853.

Bishop Balma.

He returned to the Mission, at the end of the following year; but the distemper that had apparently left him when in his native land, came back upon him a little while after his arrival in Moulmain. During his absence, affairs had been ill managed in that city. The sight of the evil which it was not in his power to remedy, coupled with the disease he was labouring under, profoundly affected his mind. The state of political affairs in Italy having had an unfortunate influence over the congregation of the Oblats, Bishop Balma saw that he could no longer expect from that quarter an accession of fellow labourers. In such extremity he made arrangements, with the consent of the Superior of the Oblats, for making over this Mission, to the Society of the Missions Etrangeres in Paris. When this was effected, Bishop

Mission made over to the French S. *des Missions Etr.*

Balma left Maulmain in November 1856, and returned to Italy.

The Rev. Gaffo after a stay of scarcely two years in the Mission, returned to Italy and died in the beginning of 1863. The Rev. Gallo remained but 18 months in Burmah, went back to Italy and thence proceeded to America where he is up to this day, discharging the functions of the sacred ministry. Brother Pasqual died at Maulmain in the year 1850. Brother Peter returned to Italy in 1857. Brother Romano is up to this year, in the capital of Burmah with father Abbona.

When Bishop Balma returned from Italy, he brought out with him two Priests, one Rev. L. Parotto who was sent to the village of Nabek. After a stay of 5 months in that place he was attacked with a complaint in his eyes which made him almost blind; he returned to Italy. The other, father Basetto, a secular Priest, not having been able to agree with his superiors, went to Calcutta, and joined the Bengal Mission.

Retrospective view of the Mission.

We must retrace our steps back and mention the arrival, in the year 1848, of three additional Priests of the Society of the Oblats, in company with the Rev. father V. Bruno, when he returned to the Burmese Mission. These were the Rev. Messrs C. Paruzza, Ch. D. Isola and D. Fornelli. The first named Priest was at first stationed in Moulmain, thence he proceeded to Bassein, with the intention of learning the Karen language and devoting himself to the mission, among the wild tribes dwelling in the neighbourhood of that town. But in 1853, he was ordered to Rangoon, to take charge of the military portion of the Catholic community. He exerted himself a great deal, in building the brick Church of St. John the Baptist, in the cantonments. Owing to a severe illness, he went to Europe for the benefit of his health in 1860, came back in 1862, and was directed to proceed to Thayetmyo, to minister to the spiritual wants of the Catholic soldiers in that station. His delicate health being unable to stand the heat of a tropical climate, he returned finally to Europe in the month of June of the following year.

Rev. Dr. Isola and Paruzza.

Rev. Fornelly.

The Rev. Fornelly was ordered to the upper country, immediately after his arrival. He laboured in the village of Nabek and Khiaungoo. He was a man of very impressionable temper; the heat of the climate sometimes affected his brains and put him in a state approaching to mental derangement. When the war broke out in 1852 between the English and the Burmese, all the European Priests were arrested, loaded with irons and dragged to the capital. Some of them were beaten and otherwise rudely handled by the Governments' satellites, for the purpose of extorting money, either from them or from their flock. The poor M. Fornelly fell in the hands of those ruffians that were of the worst character. Blows were inflicted on his person, and threats incessantly hurled at him. Such a barbarous treatment was more than sufficient to upset a head stronger than his. He lost completely his senses and became an infuriated madman. He had happily some moments of perfect mental lucidity. He died in the mission house, among his brethern, in a fit of madness in the beginning of the year 1853.

The Rev. Ch. Isola after a stay of a year or two in Maulmain, was directed to join the upper country's mission. He is now discharging the pastoral duties, in the village of Monhla.

To complete the catalogue of all the Priests of this mission, during the time that the Rev. P. P. Oblats were in charge of it, we have to mention the names of two native Priests, brought up in the College of the Propaganda at Rome.

Rev. Moses, native Priest.

The first was father Moses, a native of the village of Khiaungoo. He arrived in Burmah in 1852, at the time that war appeared imminent. He was of a weak and delicate constitution. From Amarapoora, he went to his native village to visit his relatives. He stayed there a few months. It was at that time, that the suspicious Burmese Government sent their emissaries to arrest our priests Rev. Moses, though a native of the place, was arrested with the Rev. Isola, and brought in irons to the capital. The ill treatment that he received, contributed to impair his already disordered constitution. Two or three days after his liberation, he died at Amarapoora.

The second native Priest is the Rev. G. D'Cruz born at Rangoon. After having studied for some time, the English language at Calcutta, he came back to Burmah. He expressed to Bishop Ceretti, the great desire he, had to become a Priest. His excellent dispositions having been soon duly appreciated, the good Bishop took him with himself to Europe when he returned to Italy, and placed him in the college of the Propaganda. When he had completed his studies, he was ordained Priest, and sent back to Burmah, in 1855. Father D'Cruz remained for some time in Maulmain, when he was, in the end of 1856, ordered to proceed to the Military station of Tonghoo. At that place he has given and continues to give proofs of a great zeal, and of an ardent activity for doing good and propagating the Christian religion. At last in the year 1868, he was summoned from Tonghoo, and directed to take charge of the mission's College and Press established in the town of Bassein. In that place he discharges the multifarious duties of his sacred calling, with an admirable activity, and a success truly satisfactory.

Rev. G. D'Cruz.

Since the epoch the Right Rev. Bishop Cao left the mission and the transfer of the said mission was made to the Rev. P. P. Oblats of Turin, down to the year 1856. A few occurrences happened, which must be briefly noticed, that one may have a correct idea of the situation in which the mission was during that period of about 14 years.

Let us begin with Maulmain. There was in that town a good substantial brick house for the residence of the Missionaries. That house had been built by Bishop Cao. The plank church erected by the Rev. P. Barbe in 1829, has been subsequently enlarged by the order of Dr. Ceretti, and a portico in front, was added. It was at the arrival of the fathers Oblats that the Convent was erected. It was a large plank building of a fine appearance. It served both for a paying School and an Orphanage. The building for the boys' school, was erected some time afterwards, at the expense of Mr. John Boudville. In one of the suburbs of Maulmain called Mayangoon in a southern direction, many Christian families were located, using chiefly among themselves the Burmese language. Bishop Ceretti purchased an

Account of Maulmain.

extensive piece of ground for the purpose, at first, of establishing a College. But this idea having been abandoned, a chapel was erected to which were adjoined rooms for the residence of the missionary. This is St. Mary's Church which is now nearly the same with the exception of the few improvements made at a subsequent period. At the mouth of the Salween river, stands the large village of Amherst, on the eastern bank. In that place is the station of Pilots. As several Catholic families resided in that village, a piece of ground was purchased and a small chapel erected for the celebration of the holy mysteries, when the priest from Maulmain went occasionally to visit that small congregation.

Rangoon.

In Rangoon things have remained nearly in the same state, as they were, at the departure of Bishop Cao. After the war of 1853, Bishop Balma desiring to come and fix his residence in that city, which was destined to become the capital of British Burmah, laid down in the military cantonments, the foundations of the church of St. John the Baptist. which was left in an unfinished state until the year 1857.

Bassein.

Through the exertions of the Rev. D. Tarolly, a large plank house, with a good church was erected at Bassein at the expense of an Armenian Catholic, named Joseph. In the District of Myaungmia, the same missionary who devoted himself to the conversion of the Karens, had built a very good house, a part of which was used for a chapel. The war of 1852 occasioned the total destruction of the houses and Chapels in both places, including their furniture. The same fate befell the Chapel of St. Antony, in St. John's burial ground at Rangoon, as well as the Church of the Conception, in the same city. There were, during the period under consideration, no catholic place of worship either at Thayetmyo or at Tonghoo.

Brick Church at Amarapoora.

In passing from Pegu to Burmah proper, we find that a good and substantial brick church was erected at Amarapoora, at the expense of Mr. Anthony Camaratta. The Priest's house as well as the compound were much enlarged by the exertions of Father

Abbona. In the village of Nabek a large and strong plank house was built, chiefly by the exertions of the same zealous Missionary. At Khiaungoo the Rev. Francis Bertelli rebuilt almost entirely the plank building that served both for Chapel and the residence of the Priest.

Khiaungoo.

In Monhla, the Rev. fathers Oblats built a very fine brick church at the expense of the mission. The Priest's residence was repaired and much improved by the liberality of a pious Christian lady, the widow of a Spanish gentleman, named Lanciego, formerly shabundar at Rangoon. In the large village of Khiansarua the house of the Priest, destroyed by fire, in the year 1840, was reconstructed as it now stands, as well as the fine brick church almost adjoining to it, at the expense of the widow of the same benefactor.

Monhla.

Khiansarua.

When stating the improvements made in Maulmain, by the fathers Oblats, we have omitted to mention that they had established in the mission house, a good printing Press, with sets of Burmese and Roman types. Several English books have been printed in that establishment chiefly for the use of the schools. A great number of tracts and religious publications, written in Burmese, have been issued from the same Press, by the exertions of father F. Bertelli.

Setting up of a Press.

During the period that preceded the war of 1852, the Rev. P. P. Oblats had been labouring under a very great disadvantage, in all the places under Burmese rule. Though disinclined to persecution under the pretext of religion, the Burmese rulers had always entertained the strongest suspicion against all foreigners. Any attempt from the part of the latter to penetrate into the interior of the country, and place themselves in direct communication with the natives, has always been met with either an open, or an indirect, but, not the less, a decided opposition. Many are the attempts that have been made to begin a mission among the Karens of Pegu, and the Yos, west of the village of Khiansarua, but these efforts have almost always proved abortive. When a permission was, after great and persevering efforts, obtained from some minister, or Governor of a Province, there

Position of the Mission previous to 1852.

never was a lack of delators who came to the Court, circulated the most absurd reports respecting the pretended intentions or doings of the missionaries. Upon the stress of such absurd and frivolous, ridiculous and unfounded denunciations, an order was immediately despatched, enjoining them to repair to the Capital to give an account of their conduct. When they had arrived, no further notice was taken of them, but they were given to understand that it was expected from them, that they would desist from any further attempt to penetrate into the interior of the country. These suspicious dispositions are not peculiar only to the Burmese, but they are common to all half civilized nations, in this part of the world. Indeed they are the natural offshoot of all despotic Governments in countries, where there is no constitution, and the least whim or caprice of the sovereign, is equivalent to an absolute order, which must be attended to, with the utmost punctuality. No one but he who has long resided in such countries, can have accurate notions of the fearful amount of lies, deceits, envy, and jealously that are begotten under oriental despotism. The very moral being of every individual, is thoroughly vitiated, weakened and all but destroyed. Nature and even Budhism have not implanted a spirit of intolerance in the soul of the Burmese ; on the contrary, the Natives believe that religion being essentially a part and portion of nationality, every individual has a right to follow without hindrance, or opposition the religion of the nation be belongs to. Hence the Mussulmen, the Hindoos and the Christians being looked upon as foreigners, are left at liberty to practice in the way they like, the observances of their respective creeds. They are not expected to abandon them for the Budhist observances, because the nationality they belong to, ignores Budhism. Despite such dispositions, so favorable in one respect, the position of a missionary in Burma is a very uncertain one. It is by great prudence alone, that he can succeed in keeping far from him, the suspicions of a weak, despotic, absolute, but always fearing and trembling Government. He is, however, tolerably secure, provided he limits the efforts of his zeal to the preaching of the Christian religion, to tho members of his congregations ; but the least sign of proselytism that he would give, by attempting to convert the natives, would, soon or late, bring over him the displeasure of the Government's Officers. This state of things has gradually tended to narrow the sphere of action of the missionary, and contract the efforts of his zeal. In some instances, he has limited his labours to the members of his congregation, losing sight of the secondary great object of his sacred ministry, the diffusion of the Gospel, among those who are sitting in the shade of death. In general, there have been always some conversions of Burmese, who have merged into the body of Christians. In certain instances whole families have been received in some Christian villages, and became Christians, without awaking the attention of the Officials. In this manner, despite the wars, the contagious disases, the emigration to Rangoon, the number of Christians in the villages has not become less, but has somewhat increased.

THE MISSION UNDER THE FRENCH PRIESTS OF THE CONGREGATION OF THE FOREIGN MISSIONS.

We have now to allude briefly to the causes that have prompted the transfer of the Pegu and Ava mission, to the care of the Priests of the Seminary of the Foreign missions.

Reasons for the transfer of the mission.

Since the year 1848 the Sardinian Government, aiming at the destruction of some religious bodies or corporations, published several edicts unfavorable to the Oblats in particular. The result was that the number of students gradually became less, the resources of the Congregation diminished, and it was easy to foresee that within a short space of time, the Congregation would be reduced to such extremities, that it could hold on no longer. These unfavorable circumstances indicated that soon it would be no longer in the power of the Head of the Society to send new auxiliaries to the Burmese mission. By the return, to Europe, of many missionaries, Mgr. Balma found himself unable to provide a sufficient number of Priests for the various stations where their presence was absolutely required. He knew that he had no assistance to expect from the head quarter of his Congregation. On his return to the mission in the beginning of 1855, he had brought over with him three secular priests whom he had recruited in the best way he could, but as they had apparently nothing of the genuine missionary spirit, they soon left him and the mission. Whilst he was under these painful and heart rending impressions, he wrote to the Prefect of the Propaganda to make him acquainted with the sad position of the mission, and at the same time, showing the impossibility of procuring a fresh accession of labourers. At this junction, the Bishop of the Straits, Dr. Boucho happened to be at Maulmain. He assured Dr. Balma that for his own part he would not object to the proposed plan, of making over the Burma mission to the Society of the French Foreign missions, but rather recommend it to the favorable consideration of the Directors of our Seminary. The real reason that induced the Superiors of the said Congregation to listen to the proposals made to them by the Propaganda for assuming entire charge of the Burmese mission, was the hope of opening an easy way for rapid communication, with our missions in Western China, and particularly that of Yunan.

The Coadjutor of the latter mission, Mgr. Chauveau had contrived to send from Talifoo, to the city of Amarapoora, in 1854, some Christians, who were well received by the king, and carried back with them, some presents from his Majesty to the Bishop. Subsequently another deputation of Christians reached the same destination, and safely returned to Yunan. The communications with that province *via* Canton were lengthy, unsafe and very expensive. The difference between the two routes was so great and so much in favor of the route *via* Amarapoora, that Mgr. Chauveau, by his letters endeavoured to call and fix the attention of the Council of the Seminary of Foreign missions upon this most important point. It was just at this time, that the Cardinal Prefect of the Propaganda, proposed to our Congregation to take charge of the Burmese mission. The answer that was first sent to Rome, was couched in very respectful terms of perfect submission to the order of the eminent Prelate, but, at the same time, he was informed that our congregation had already a very extensive field to cultivate in various parts of the Peninsula of India, and of Indo China, and that they thought it would be perhaps an act of imprudence from their part, to accept the charge of a new mission. This answer was forwarded in the beginning of 1855, and its particulars made known in Penang in the month of September of the same year. Mgr. Balma, at the same time, was writing fresh letters to the Cardinal Prefect urging him not to delay in making over the mission to some Congregation which would be both able and willing to cultivate the portion of the vineyard, he could no longer take care of. Upon the receipt of these letters, the Head of the council of the Propaganda, pressed on the Superior of the seminary of Foreign missions the acceptance of the mission of Ava and Pegu. This happened at the end of the year 1855. The mission of Malesia was to supply both the superior and about four or five missionaries for the newly incorporated mission. This small number was thought sufficient for the time being, as it was hoped that the Rev. P. P. Oblats would continue to remain in the mission, at least for some years longer.

The new Superior.

When the news of the formal acceptation reached Penang, no time was lost in making the preliminary arrangements for carrying out the intentions of the sacred Congregation.

The very Rev. Paul Ambrose Bigandet, pro-vicar of the Malesia mission, on account of his knowledge of the Burmese language, was appointed Superior of the new mission, which was *de jure* connected with the Malesia mission, though *de facto*, completely separated from it. In the beginning of January 1856 the Rev. M. Lacramp was sent from Penang to Maulmain, to settle some affairs with Bishop Balma and make him acquainted with the early coming of his successor.

Consecrated Bishop at Penang.

The future superior was consecrated at Penang Bishop of Ramatha, *inpartibus Infidilium*, on the 30th of March, of the same year, with the title of administrator of the Pegu and Ava mission, and Coadjutor to the Vicar Apostolic of the Straits. On the 4th of April he left Penang, on board of the Steamer *Pluto*, with the Rev. P. Barbe and the Rev. X. Ducotey. Having arrived at Mergui, at the mouth of the Tenasserim, he was joined by the Rev. R. Naude and, on the 14th April, he reached Maulmain.

Leaves Penang with Bishop Ducotey and Barbe, is joined by father Nande.

Dr. Balma was then in that city with the Rev. G. D'Cruz. He was lying very ill of dysentry. The poor Bishop had been unable to attend to any business for several months, so that his Successor found himself at once burdened with the management of all affairs, without any one, who could tender him some advice to enlighten his mind on the state, affairs were in. He had to grope his way as well as he could. The temporal affairs of the mission were in the worst possible condition. They had been handled for the last two or three years successively by unskilful hands and unwise heads. Instead of finding some funds wherewith to provide for the current necessities and wants, there were heavy debts both in Maulmein and Rangoon. Moreover the destructive results of the late war were sadly conspicuous in all the stations of Pegu, and in Burma proper. From every part, demands were made, wants were exposed, assistance was asked, but there were no means at hand. Not a rupee had been allowed to the Head of the mission for meeting the contingencies of his position. He was left alone, to himself and to his own resources, and told coolly by those who were bound to afford him aid, to manage in the best way he could to extricate himself from the difficulties that encompassed him and the troubles that heavily pressed on him.

Difficulties of the Bishop's position.

After a stay of about 25 days in Maulmain, the new Bishop hastened to visit the different stations in Pegu, and personally make himself acquainted with the real state of things. Previous to his leaving Maulmain, he appointed the Rev. X. Ducoty, to be the officiating Priest at that important station. Thence he went to Rangoon. That town, as far as the affairs of the church were concerned, was in a most miserable position. There was only a bamboo building; two thirds of which served for a church, and the other third was used for the residence of the priests. Four days after the Bishop's arrival, that miserable building was blown down by the wind. The new church in the cantonment, was half finished, and of the three rooms occupied by the clergyman, only one was finished, and fit for habitation. It was there that the Bishop had to accommodate himself and the four Priests that were with him, in the best way he could.

He visits the Rangoon Mission.

Bassein and Myaungmia.

The monsoon was just setting in, when the Bishop went, in a boat, to visit the Karen stations of Myaungmia, under the mangement of Rev. D. Tarolly. He was much comforted and rejoiced at the progress religion had made among those children of the forest. Having spent eight days in that place, he continued his voyage with the same companion, the Rev. Lacrampe, to Bassein, where he found the Rev. V. Gabutti, living in a poor room behind the Chapel, that had been erected after the war with the materials supplied from some ruined Burmese monastery. In that place there was a small detachment of European troops, and a small Karen congregation, the members of which dwelt in some neighbouring villages Two months afterwards, the Rev. Gabutti being ill, a change was deemed necessary. The Rev. R. Naude went to relieve him. The above named missionary went to Maulmain, to take charge of the congregation of Mayangon. The Rev. Lacrampe being well acquainted with the Karen language, went in the jungle and began a mission among the Karens, at a small distance from Bassein.

He visits Thayetmyo with Father Barbe.

On his return to Rangoon, the Bishop was joined by the Rev. P. Barbe. He resolved to go with him to visit the stations of the mission of Upper Burma. They left Rangoon, on the 15th of August, in a Government Steamer. On their way, they visited the military station of Thayetmyo, where the Rev. C. Pachiotti was officiating, and ministering to the spiritual wants of the Catholic soldiers belonging to that station. After a stay of 10 days in that place, the Bishop went up to Amarapoora, then the Capital of Burma. The King graciously received him and allowed him three elephants to go and visit the five Christian villages, in the west of the capital, beyond the river Irrawaddy. A little more than a month was employed on that visitation tour. He returned to Amarapoora and arrived in that city on the 1st of November. Soon after having obtained from the King, the permission to proceed to Bhamo, the Bishop with Father Barbe left Amarapoora in a very comfortable boat, kindly supplied to him by His Majesty's order. The object of this voyage was one of great concern for the mission of Western

Proceeds to Amarapoora. Kindly received by the King.

Voyage to Bhamo.

China. It was intended to ascertain whether it were practicable to open regular communications between Burma and the western part of the Province of Yunan. Many letters previously received from Mgr. Chauveau, the Coadjutor of the Vicar Apostolic of Yunan, gave strong grounds of hope for securing that most desirable result.

State of the Country.

Bhamo was safely reached in the month of November. That time was precisely the season of the arrival of the Chinese Caravans. But in that year they did not make their appearance. Some people pretended that the Kakhiyns inhabiting the chain of mountains between China and Burma, had refused to allow the Caravans to pass. But the real cause of this unexpected disappointment, was the war that had begun to rage between the Panthays (mussulmen inhabiting Yunan) and the Chinese. The same cause has up to this day, prevented our missionaries in Yunan, from communicating freely with us.

Another untoward and unfavorable influence has been brought to bear upon us, for rendering any attempt at opening communications, almost impossible. The Chinese trade with Burma is entirely in the hands of a company of merchants, residing at Talifoo and another town of western Yunan. That Company has a chief agent in the Burmese capital. They have enjoyed for many years, the sole monopoly of that trade. They are averse at seeing Europeans endeavouring to find out the road that they follow. They do their utmost to thwart them in all their efforts to open communication with China in that direction, lest the monopoly they have hitherto enjoyed, be wrested from their hands. In the year 1861, Bishop Chauveau had sent some Christian Chinese with goods for trade, to Mandalay; but they were all murdered and their goods plundered in the neighbourhood of Bhamo. It appears probable that the Burmese joined the Chinese in the perpetration of this diabolical deed.

Information on the road to Yunan.

During his stay at Bhamo, the Bishop made every effort to obtain accurate information respecting the road followed by the Chinese Caravans. From the conflicting accounts that were given to him, he gathered the following items of information. On leaving Bhamo, travellers enter into the gorges of mountains, the

7

passes of which are in the hands of the tribe of Singphos, called Kakhyins by the Burmese, and it takes them three days to cross the whole range. They penetrate into less mountainous districts, inhabited by the Shans, who are nominally tributary to the Chinese, and after a four days' march, they reach the first Chinese town called Maumien, so that it takes seven days to go from Bhamo to the Chinese frontier. From thence to Talifoo, the distance is only six or eight days. The passage through the Kakhyin hills is difficult, because these people are divided into several clans, which endeavour to annoy travellers and levy on them taxes as much as they can obtain, partly by threats, and partly by force. There are also some places reputed to be very unhealthy. Travellers ought carefully to avoid spending a night in those localities, or drink of the water therein found. Perhaps the safest way to insure the safety of non-Chinese travellers, would be to obtain through the King of Burma, from the Chinese Company's Agent a sort of safe conduct, stating that he would be responsible for any harm that might be done to the adventurous travellers.

Situation of Bhamo.

The situation of Bhamo, on the eastern bank of the Irrawaddy is a very pleasant and agreeable one. Between the town and the foot of the mountains, there is a vast plain almost entirely uncultivated, of four or five miles in extent. What renders the town so unhealthy, is a large and deep ditch, with several ramifications, full during the greatest part of the year, of stagnant water, from which pestilential exhalations are rising, spreading, all about the germ of fevers of the worst description. Very little labour, could open an issue with the river and thereby relieve the inhabitants of the town from malignant fevers that periodically infest the place. The town is surrounded by a wooden palissade on all sides, except the one that is washed by the river. The number of houses was not above 600, and those in general of a very poor description. The chinese joss house is the only building that has a tolerably decent appearance. Bhamo is naturally the rendezvous of all the Tribes living in those remote localities. Were the place under the management of a prudent and wise administration, it would become what it was in former times, the Emporium of a large, extensive and lucrative trade.

Formerly a great Emporium of trade.

As a missionary station, Bhamo would stand unrivalled. Every day, the missionary could come in contact with individuals belonging to various tribes, converse with them, make himself acquainted with all that has a reference to their manners and habits, and gradually make them acquainted with the vivifying and consoling truths of our holy Religion. With ordinary precautions and common prudence, a European could keep his health and be able to discharge with perfect safety the duties of his calling. The neighboring hills on the East and West, are peopled with several clans of Kakhyins. The Shans are to be found in every direction, but all of them are Budhists, as well as the largest portion of the Paloongs Tribe. But the Kakhyins and the other wild tribes are untainted with the religion of Budha. They have a sort of geniolatry, which constitutes the whole of their religion. The Kakhyins are represented as a wicked and treacherous race. I believe there is some foundation in this bad opinion that is entertained respecting them. Many instances of their cruel dispositions may be but too true. They are fond of making raids in the districts of their neighbours and enslaving all the people they can seize. But it must be admitted that the way they have been often treated by the unscrupulous Burmese, and the cunning Chinese, has not a little contributed to make an alteration in their natural dispositions and to engraft on their better nature, vices of a foreign growth. Be that as it may, the Kakhyins offer a fine and extensive field to the zeal of missionaries animated with the true spirit of their vocation. It seems to me that they ought to be the first object to attract the serious attention of an active and enterprising servant of God, and enlist the affections of his heart. The day, the writer trusts, is not far, when the members of that tribe will have the gladenning news of the Gospel announced to them.

Return to Amarapoora.

After a stay of 15 days in Bhamo, the Bishop was supplied, by the Governor with a comfortable boat, to return to Amarapoora, which place was reached a few days before Christmas. On the second of January 1857, having obtained from the liberality of the King, three Elephants, the Bishop in company, with the Rev. P. Barbe, set out from the Royal city, shaping his course in a southern direction, towards Tonghoo, which was reached on the 17th of the same month. The road he followed was not very bad: it is leading from Ava all along the foot of the chain of hills, stretching in a southerly direction as far as Mehau. The only places of some importance that are met with are Yemethin and Ningian, which give their name to two provinces.

Departure from Amerapoora to Tonghoo.

Tonghoo was formerly the capital of an independent kingdom; but it was reduced to the condition of a Burmese province, since the fall of the Pegu Monarchy. It is now the place which may be considered as the first military station in the North East, on the border of countries inhabited by wild tribes.

Tonghoo.

There the Bishop found the Rev. G. D'Cruz giving with zeal, the benefit of his sacred ministry to the Catholic soldiers belonging to that station. No church had yet been erected. The Priest lived in a poor bamboo house; and an old barrack served for a church.

Here is a circumstance, which the writer thinks is worthy to be recorded. During the voyage down the Tsitang river, the mind of the Bishop was in a state of great depression, owing to the pecuniary difficulties in which he saw the mission involved. He could not see by what means he could extricate it from its present embarrassment. Being asked by his companion, what could be the cause of his unusual and ill-disguised mental anguishes, the Bishop plainly told him the real cause of the change he remarked in him. The good father Barbe after a moment of reflection, said: " For all kind of sickness, there is a remedy. Here is the remedy I propose for the present emergency. Let the sum of 15,000 francs, be borrowed from our Seminary in Paris, to be repaid in three instalments of 5,000 a year. In this way it will be possible to meet all pressing difficulties." This simple advice was a flash of light in the Bishop's mind. He acted up to this suggestion, and thanks be to God, all difficulties have gradually disappeared. The financial position of the mission has soon improved. The missionaries have all shown on this occasion, the greatest disinterestedness and a readiness to put up cheerfully with all privations, in order to help the common cause.

After a fortnight's stay at Tonghoo, the Bishop came down to Shwegyin and Sittang towns, then with small garrisons on the eastern bank of the Sittang river. He then crossed over the tongue of land separating the Sittang and Pegu rivers, and reached the old city of Pegu, the former capital of the Kingdom of that name. There he took again passage on board of a boat, and reached Rangoon at the end of February 1857. He thus completed the tour of visitation of the whole mission, including the voyage to and from Bhamo, in six months and a half.

Visits Shwegyin, Sittang and Pegu.

During that period, a mission house had been erected in the town of Rangoon, and on his return, the Bishop, at last, found a place to live in. Likewise a small little chapel had been erected on the ground of St. John, which was absolutely sufficient for the present wants of a small congregation. But what was still more consoling, was the arrival of three young Missionaries from France in October 1856. They landed at Maulmein. They were, the Rev. A. Lecomte, F. Guerin and P. Dumollard. The former, agreeably to the orders received from his Superior, came over to Rangoon in the month of November 1856. The second went to Toungoo to assist the Rev. D'Cruz and together with him to promote the interest of religion, in that remote station. The third was appointed to the Church of Mayangon, near Maulmein, in place of the Rev. V. Gabutti who came over to Rangoon to assist the Rev. father Paruzza, in the Military Cantonment Church.

Arrival of Rev. Dumollard, Guerin, and Lecomte.

In Maulmein, the affairs of the mission had been for a long period, in a deplorable condition. The girls and boys school were sadly neglected and had fallen in a state of undescribable confusion.

The Rev. X. Ducoty laboured with a great zeal, and much success in replacing both institutions on a better footing. A substantial plank building was erected for receiving the orphan girls who hitherto, had been crowded in the lower part of the convent. The course of studies was much improved, and in a short time, the fruit of his praiseworthy exertions, became most conspicuous. The same

Education received a fresh impulse at Maulmein.

beneficial results attended his efforts in setting the Boys school on a good footing. Mayangon likewise was not neglected The Rev. P. Dumollard contrived to induce one of his parishioners, M. Ramos, to erect a neat little building designed for a girls' school.

Revolt of a few Karens which leads to the establishment of the Kanazogon station.

Whilst these improvements were happily going on in Maulmein, Providence offered an excellent opportunity in the midst of the Pegu province for propagating Christian religion among the Karens In the district of Shoaylaung, there appeared a fanatical Karen who gave himself as a *Min-laung* or a personage destined to become a King. He craftily practised on the credulity and simplicity of the Karens, and persuaded many to become his followers. He assumed the air of a prince, with the paraphernalia of his dignity and began to roam over the district in order to increase the number of his adherents. Many simple Karens were taken in, by his deceitful language and promises. The incipient insurrection as a matter of course, was soon put down, and the chief actor was arrested and safely lodged in the Bassein jail. The Burmese who were employed as chiefs in the disturbed district, began to arrest and annoy all the Karen population, for the ostensible object of showing their zeal in defending the interests of the English Government, but principally for securing to themselves large sums of money that were easily extorted from the poor persecuted Karens, under the pretence of releasing them from all trouble and vexation. The Rev. A. Lacrampe happened to be in that district at the very time that the poor Karens were indiscriminately hunted like wild beasts. Only but a few, were his disciples who had begun to learn the elements of Christian religion. The others, in the hope of finding protection, flung themselves into his arms, promising to obey him and do whatever he would command them. In a short time, the number of Neophytes rapidly increased to several hundreds. The seat of the new congregation was established on a well selected spot, called Kanazogon, nearly half way between Shoaylaung and Miaungmya. At first a long building was raised by the Karens which was used in part for the priest's residence, but the larger portion was reserved for divine service. The number of Christians increasing, it was thought advisable to build a substantial plank church apart, and a house for the residence of priests. These two buildings together with a third one for the schools were all completed in 1862. They have a fine appearance and will likely last for a great number of years. In the end of the above mentioned year, the number of Christians rose to a little more than one thousand.

Rev. Bertrand and Tagnet.

In the beginning of the year 1858, the Mission received a fresh accession of labourers in the persons of the Rev. P. Tagnet and P. Bertrand. The latter father went to Kanazogon to assist father Lacrampe, learn the Karen language, and qualify himself for the duties of Missionary among the wild inhabitants of the forests of Pegu. The former was directed to proceed to Miaungmia and, under the auspices of the Rev. D. Tarolly, to prepare himself to become a fellow labourer in the same field. When father Tagnet knew a little of Karen, Father Tarolly came to establish himself in a place called Giawine, in the neighbourhood of Rangoon on the western bank of the river.

Rev. Tarolly settles at Shaboua then Kiaongwine.

Brick Church in Maulmain.

In the beginning of the year 1857, the corner stone of the brick church of Maulmain was laid down with great solemnity, by Mr. F. Narcis one of the oldest Christian inhabitants of that town. Mr. Phillips, a wealthy merchant of the place, undertook to defray all the expenses to be incurred for the erection of the Church, but he died suddenly of an apoplectic stroke, in the middle of the year 1858, without having made his will. The work was far from completion ; but the Rev. X. Ducoty by his energetic exertions, contrived to find means for carrying on the work, and the church under the invocation of St. Patrick, was solemnly blessed and opened for divine service, by the Bishop, in February 1859.

Brick Church in Rangoon.

In February 1858, the corner stone of the church of Rangoon was laid down amidst a great concourse of people. The ceremony was presided by the Bishop, assisted by the Rev. P. Barbe, C. Paruzza, C. Pacchiotti and V. Gabutti. The band of the European Regiment enlivened the ceremony. M. Th. Chrestian laid down the corner stone. During the rainy season, the work was interrupted, to give time to the foundations to sit well in the ground.

The work was resumed in the month of October, and carried on without interruption. The church was blessed and, for the first time, opened for divine service on the 3rd Sunday of Advent, of the year 1859. It was erected solely at the expense of Mr. Gregory Avanis an Armenian, native of Rangoon who since the war of 1824 had migrated to Madras, where he died on the 2nd of April 1858 having just received the information that the work of laying the foundation of the church, had been begun.

He bequeathed a sum of 20,000 rupees, for building the church, and a similar sum in Company's papers, with the injunction that the interest should be used for repairing the church, and praying for the repose of his soul.

Christian Brothers in Maulmain.

In the year 1859, father Ducoty contrived to obtain the valuable assistance of the Christian Brothers for keeping up the Boys' School in Maulmain. Three of them came at first, and a fourth one followed not long after. The upper part of the school room, as well as the lower part were much improved, but it was in the year 1862 that the building was enlarged and fitted out for the lodgement of the Brothers and their boarders.

Girls' school in Rongoon.

By the care of the Bishop, a large piece of ground had been secured in 1857, in the ancient burying ground of St. John's for the purpose of establishing an Institution intended for the education of young ladies, and an orphanage, for receiving poor children, who otherwise would be left in a state of complete destitution and reserved to a worse state when grown up. In the month of August of the year 1860, the building for the education of young ladies, was begun, and completed in the month of April of the following year. Two Sisters from Maulmain with a young lady came in May, and on the first of June opened the School which under God's blessing has prospered despite the great difficulties that had to beovercome Mr Domingo Lewis has assisted the Bishop in getting up the Institution, with a liberal donation of six thousand Rupees. The total expense has reached to nearly double that sum. In the year 1862, the orphanage was begun, and completed in the beginning of the following year, together with all the out-offices, and the wall about the compound. It is large enough to accommodate fifty or seventy orphan girls.

Christian Brothers Rangoon.

Whilst these works were going on, the Bishop was not unmindful of the education of boys. He was anxious to provide for the benefit of the rising generation of male children, a boon similar to that conferred on the Catholic community of Maulmain. In 1861 a small community of Christian Brothers was installed in Rangoon, and during the course of that year, a large building was erected for them in the compound of the church. All the out-offices were placed in another compound, separated from it by a small 30 feet road. This school has prospered exceedingly. The number of the boys has much increased. It is so great now, that the school premises are by far too narrow and quite insufficient to accommodate comfortably the ever increasing number of pupils.

Rebuilding of the Church at Mergui.

But whilst mentioning the improvements, almost simultaneously taking place in Rangoon and Maulmain, let us not lose sight of the good that was done in another quarter, at Mergui the southernmost station of the mission. In 1856 the church and mission house had been totally destroyed by fire. The Rev. M. Renier had no place to live in, but a small bamboo house, hastily erected after the fire. In the following year a good plank house was made, a portion of which was set apart for divine service. In the year 1862 a good church was built at the expense of Mr. G. D'Castro, on the very spot occupied by the former church. It is in every respect, similar to the one that was built about forty years ago by a native priest, the Rev. father John, and I believe that the same kind benefactor, Mr. George D'Castro bore the greatest part, if not the whole of the expense. Mr. George D'Castro is well entitled to the distinctive and honorific appellation of *Kiaung taga*, bestowed by the Burmese on those who by their liberality, build a church or a priest house.

Father Naude at Bassein.

In the year 1858, the Rev. M. Naude, who during many years had devoted his zeal and energy to the Karen mission of the Tenasserim coast, was sent temporarily to Bassein to examine what post would offer the most

8

favorable chances of success in the Karen forests. During severa-months, he laboured with a great zeal in Bassein and did much good among the poor Karens who were detained in the Bassein jail. Providence brought him in contact with a karen prisoner, whose relatives lived in the Henzadah district. He appeared to be a man of some influence among his countrymen. By the application of the good missionary to the chief of the Bassein district, the days of this man's imprisonment were shortened, and as soon as he was set at liberty, be offered to accompany father Naude to his village. The proposal was accepted and both were soon on their way to that place. The man at first proved faithless, but nevertheless, he had been in the hands of Providence, the means of setting on foot the establishment of a mission in those parts. Despite the great and appalling difficulties that beset in every direction the servant of Christ, father Naude succeeded by his perseverance, and confidence in God, in establishing himself firmly in those parts. Now he is at the head of a Karen congregation numbering more than 1,100 souls with a very good house, a strong and well built Church, and a school house for the boys. This part of the Karen mission is very promising, and under God's blessing, there is every hope to see the various stations constituting the Henzadah Mission, making greater developments.

Death of father Polignani.

Amongst the members of the mission, death has made great havoc during the short space of three years. The very Revd. N. Polignani, Vicar general of the Upper Burmah Mission, had laboured in those parts during the long period of 28 years. He had arrived in the Mission in the year 1831. His first destination was China, but on his arrival at Macao, his Superior knowing the troubled condition of that part of the Chinese empire where was the mission under his management, thought it necessary to change the destination of the Revd. Polignani. He was directed to proceed to the Burmese Mission. His stay has always been in the Upper Country and chiefly in the village of Khiansarua. He had come in November 1859 to meet the Bishop at Mandalay. He was then in perfect health. He left the capital on the 9th of November together with the Bishop. He parted company with him near Nabek, and went to that village. He thence proceeded to

Khiaungoo. During the way, he was seized with an attack of cholera, and expired a few hours after having reached that village, on the 3rd of December. Father Polignani was a Napolitan and belonged to the Benedictine order. He was, indeed, the pattern of a genuine Missionary. His zeal, the cheerful disposition of his temper, the love he bore to his spiritual children, the tender care he bestowed on their souls and bodies, the perfect regularity of his private life, are the glorious mementos he has left behind him, which will perpetuate his memory, for many years to come, in the Christian villages of Upper Burmah.

Arrival and death of Revd. Martin.

In 1860 the Revd. Martin reached Rangoon, in the month of April. But unfortunately he was labouring under the incurable distemper of consumption, and he died in the following September.

Death of Revd. Barbe.

In 1861 the Revd. P. Barbe was seized with an attack of dysentry, whilst on his way to the South of Mergui. The disease for a month or two appeared to have subsided, but in the middle of May, it suddenly re-appeared with the very worst signs. After a short illness, the patient calmly expired at Rangoon. Father Barbe was the veteran of the Mission. He had arrived in the Malayan Mission in 1826. He subsequently laboured in the Bengal Mission, at Calcutta and Chittagong. He then re-entered the Malayan Mission, and when the Burmese mission was made over to the Priests of the congregation of foreign missions, he followed the new Bishop and remained a member of this mission until his death. The best part of his property he left at the disposal of the executor of his will, to be employed in such good works as would appear to him most suitable and appropriate. It was chiefly with the money he had left, that the buildings of St. Peter's Institute, at Bassein, were erected.

Arrival of father Bernard.

These losses were in part compensated, by the arrival of father N. Bernard, who after some years of fruitless attempts to penetrate into Thibet *via* Assam, and *via* Simla, was directed by the Superior of the Seminary Paris, to join the Burmese mission. He did so in 1859. Two years after, three new Missionaries arrived from France, Revd. Messrs. Tardivel, Chevillon, and Devos. The first was directed to go to the Henzadah district, and assist the Revd. M. Naude. The second proceeded to Maulmain, and assumed charge of St. Mary's Church, Mayangon. The third went to Kanazogon, to study the Karen language with Revd. P. Bertrand, and qualify himself for the duties of a missionary among the Karens.

Rebuilding of the church at Nabeck.

In the year 1858, the Church of Nabeck being in a ruinous condition, the lower parts of the posts entirely rotten and eaten up by the white ants, it was deemed absolutely necessary to rebuild it anew. Father Polignani thought it would be better to have it made of bricks. He laid down the foundation in the beginning of the above named year. The work went on rather slowly and the edifice was not completed before the year 1861, when father Lecomte put a finishing hand to it. It was blessed with great solemnity by the Bishop assisted by the very Revd. P. Abbona and Revd. Lecomte and Sub-deacon Dominico Tessio, on the 19th October. A great number of Christians had come from the royal city to be present at the ceremony. The pagans from the neighbourhood crowded the place on the occasion and behaved with perfect regularity. A few days after the blessing of the new Church, the Revd. D. Tessio, at first a lay brother of the Oblats Order, had been ordained subdeacon in the church of Mandalay. He was subsequently promoted to the order of Deacon, and two days afterwards, elevated to the Priesthood. He had acted as catechist in the village of Khiaungio, and given great satisfaction to his superiors, by his irreproachable conduct and his zeal in teaching the christians of the locality he had been placed in charge of. These two-fold considerations induced the Bishop to raise him to the priestly dignity.

Ordination of Revd. Tessio.

Father Lecomte in the Upper country.

We have omitted to mention the various circumstances that brought father Lecomte from Rangoon to Nabeck. Whilst dwelling in the former place he was attacked with a chronic dysentry of the very worst description. All the remedies administered by European physicians had availed nothing. The Bishop thought that a voyage up the Irrawaddy would likely prove beneficial to the patient. After a stay of some months the patient found himself much better and soon was restored to the enjoyment of his health. When the Bishop was at Mandalay in 1859, the King urgently pressed him to give to him the Revd. Lecomte for the education of his children, and of those of his brother, the heir apparent. The request was granted, though with a certain amount of reluctance, based upon the little hope entertained of the realization of this plan. Revd. father Lecomte came to Rangoon, for taking up the school furniture he wanted, and purchasing what was necessary for the future establishment. After having completed his purchases, he returned in all haste to Mandalay. But the mind of the King had already undergone some changes, owing to the influence of the Phongies, and perhaps of the women of the palace. He would send to the school only some of the boys, who are loitering day and night in the palace. As the Missionary had positive orders from his superior not to hold a school except for the benefit of the King's sons, he declined his Majesty's offer, and after a lapse of some months, he was directed to proceed to Nabeck and assume charge of the congregation of that village, together with that of Khiaungoo. Moreover, father Abbona having on several occasions showed a desire to return to Europe, father Lecomte was desired to remain in the upper country, for the purpose of occupying the post of Missionary in the royal city after the departure of father Abbona.

The new site of the Church Khiaungoo.

The village of Khiaungoo is of all other christian localities, the one that has suffered most in both a temporal and spiritual point of view, from causes that shall be enumerated hereafter. It was there, too, that the Bishop directed chiefly his attention, in order to put on a better footing that Christian congregation. The compound actually occupied by the church was in many respects very unsuitable. Revd. Lecomte pointed out a very eligible spot in its vicinity. But there was a great obstacle in the way. About twelve or fifteen houses tenanted by Pagans, occupied part of the contemplated ground. They were most of them unwilling to remove their houses anywhere else, though a very reasonable compensation was offered to them. The chief of the place through fear, did not like to press these people and make them feel the weight of his authority. The last chance of success that remained was to make an application to the King. Fortunately in 1862 the Bishop was then at Mandalay, with the English Chief Commissioner of British Burmah. The latter was busily engaged in negotiating a Treaty with His Majesty. The Bishop had, then, the opportunity, of rendering some services to both parties on the occasion. He profited by this favorable opportunity, to petition the King for obtaining the ground at Khiaungoo. His demand was most graciously received by the King, who ordered the chief of the district to cause the burmese houses to be removed, and surround the compound with a good and substantial fence. A compensation was to be paid to the Burmese, and the fence made at the King's expense. The building which had hitherto been used for the Chapel, and the missionary's residence were then removed in the new compound, and trusting in the aid of Providence, a good and substantial brick church will be soon erected in that place.

Improvements at Khiansarua.

In the large village of Khiansarua, some improvements have likewise taken place. The said village is divided into two parts called the North and South villages, separated by an extensive paddy field, belonging to the Burmese. When the Bishop visited that place, in 1860, he saw the importance of purchasing that piece of ground, for giving more extension to the village, particularly in the southern division, where the houses are crowded within too narrow limits. After many *pour parlers*, the owners at last parted with the field for the sum of 300 Rupees. One half was paid by the Bishop and the other half, by the congregation.

On that ground close to the Christian burial, there was a little spot where the Burmese of the neighbourhood were in the habit of bringing their dead bodies to be cremated. Father Andreino, by a bold step prevailed also upon the Burmese to select somewhere else another spot for the cremation of the dead. Now the whole belongs entirely to the Christians and is free from any servitude from the part of the Pagans.

Vernacular school in Upper Burmah.

In all the villages, there are schools, for the boys and girls, who have thus an opportunity, of learning to read, write and acquire a good knowledge of the rudiments of Christian religion. These schools do a great deal of good, but the sphere of their usefulness could be much enlarged. They are too much on the native system, that is to say, the masters of these small institutions, are unfit to convey instruction in a manner calculated to develop the mind and give energy to its faculties. They follow a kind of routine, by which children are taught the art of reading and writing, by a process almost similar to that used for teaching animals to play some part they are not led by their instinct to perform. The result of this disastrous mode of proceeding in the training of youth, is made apparent in the intercourse one has with grown up men. There is a total deficiency of thought and reflection. No effort is ever made for considering a subject, comparing it with another, and drawing a conclusion which forms the basis of a real conviction. The faculty of memory is alone heavily tasked in the studies of pupils. They learn by heart sometimes an astonishing number of words, but the teacher never takes the trouble to explain anything to show the relations between one idea and another, to lead the lad to draw an inference. The knowledge they acquire is purely mechanical instead of being a well prepared food for the intellect. In fact the capabilities, nay the very existence of the mind is practically ignored by the pretended teachers of youth. This capital defect is in the opinion of the writer, the real cause of the supineness of mind remarked, by even superficial observers, as characteristic of the Indo eastern nations, the imitative turn of their genius and their utter incapability of originating anything. Should the Birmans be taken as an instance of the correctness of the foregoing remarks, we see that in their religion, plays, literature etc. everything is clothed in the Hindu attire, with nothing to veil the original features, but the language. They have been so, for the last fifteen hundred years, and they will in all probability remain in the same state of fixity for an incalculable period, unless some effort be made for giving to the mind a full scope of development. When the mind shall have been properly worked upon, then the Burmese will arise from that state of torpor, and awake from their mental slumbering and be capacitated to distinguish between the secular errors in which they have been plunged, and the truths that shall be offerred to them. But enough upon a subject of such a melancholy nature. The practical conclusion to be inferred from the foregoing remarks, is that a better mode of conveying the rudiments of knowledge, must be adopted in the schools, under the supervision of the missionaries. The writer is aware of the many difficulties the missionaries have to contend with, for carrying a reform on that important and vital subject, but sufficient to say that such difficulties are not insuperable. Every one must set hard at work to successfully overcome them.

Normal school at Bassein.

For the purpose of remedying the evil just complained of, and preventing its growth and spread in the rising Karen missions, the Bishop had long entertained the idea of establishing at Bassein, a school or seminary, placed under the immediate supervision of a European Missionary, for the purpose of educating young Karens and Burmese, and by communicating to them a good amount of knowledge, and training them up in the rational way that is observed in well managed schools in Europe ; and thereby to prepare them for discharging effectually the important duties of school masters and Catechists. The Superior had fixed his eyes upon the Revd. P. Dumollard, as eminently qualified for this duty. But during more than two years, several untoward occurrences thwarted the execution of the plan, and prevailed the Revd. gentleman from being sufficiently disengaged to second the view of the head of the Mission. At last in the year 1861, he repaired to Bassein for the purpose of making the preliminary arrangements. The locality as far as the compound is concerned, is vast, and well fitted for an Institution ; but the small and old buildings were unsuitable for admitting a certain num- of boys. The Revd. Dumollard was not a man to be disheartened by such difficulties. He collected about twelve or fifteen boys, from the two principal Karen stations, and forthwith began the good work with a praiseworthy earnestness. Soon after a good opportunity having afforded the means of procuring three Christian Brothers, the Bishop thought that they would form most excellent auxiliaries for keeping up the Bassein school, and enlarging the sphere of its usefulness by extending the blessing of education to a certain number of boys of the town. During the winter of the year 1862, the out-offices of the new institution were built of masonry, and a good place for the printing press. Meanwhile the building of the Institution was begun and carried on with great vigor. It would have been soon finished, had not a misfortune caused the raft upon which were accumulated all the ready materials for the house, to split into two parts, occasioning thereby a great loss of a valuable portion of the posts and planks. But the energy of Father Dumollard soon repaired the losses, and the building has been completed in the month of July of the present year. The number of boarders in the Institution, amounts to sixty-two, besides a similar number of children from the town.

New Church at Tounghoo.

The progress the good cause has made at Toungoo, under the zealous management, of Father D'Cruz, deserves a special notice. When the Revd. gentleman reached Tonghoo, there was no place appropriated for divine service. The holy mysteries were performed in a dilapidated and half ruined old barrack. In the year 1858 the Government gave the sum of 7,000 Rupees, towards helping to build a Church for the use of the Catholic soldiers at that Station. With that sum, a new church has been erected on the very walls of the ancient city, in a conspicuous position close to the boundaries of the military cantonment. The building is a very neat one, and reflects great credit on the missionary who has planned and executed it. By husbanding with economy the resources at his disposal, he has found a sufficient remnant of the Government's money for supplying the Church with fine furniture. Whilst the zealous Missionary bestowed the greatest care on the Catholics of that Station, he found sufficient time to preach to the Shans, who had emigrated from their country and had come to settle in the territory of Tonghoo. He has converted about 20 families which he has located on a good spot of ground near the banks of the river. There they form a small village and cultivate the ground for their maintenance. Moreover some Burmese families have also heard the good news and increased the native Church in that district.

The want of a church was much felt, in the royal city of Mandalay. After the removal of the people from Amarapoora to Mandalay, in 1857, the Revd. P. Abbona had first to concern himself in securing for the Christians and for the church, two excellent spots of ground. He hastened to erect a good and substantial house for the dwelling of the missionary. A portion of the house was set apart for a church or place of worship, which was used until the year 1863. With his usual energy and activity he laid down during the previous year, the foundations of a good and substantial Church. The foundations are of brick, raised about four feet above the level of the ground. Upon them stands a strongly and elegantly built church, with a plank roof and a broad verandah running all round it. By his great exertions, father Abbona has procured from different quarters, the funds necessary to defray the considerable expense incurred on this occasion. The King being friendly disposed towards the Mission, gave the best part of the funds required ; but the Revd. father had to find the remaining, among his Christians and the few foreigners residing in the Capital. The church was blessed by the Bishop, in the month of April 1863.

New Church at Mandalay.

There already existed in that same locality, a girls school under the charge of a native mistress. In that school a certain number of poor orphan girls were living as boarders, in a portion of the building. If not finely housed, they were at least rescued from the perils that awaited them, if left unprovided for. The sphere of usefulness of such an Institution was very limited, both on account of the narrowness of the place and the incapacity of the mistress. Father Abbona set at work to build a large house for the accommodation of three Sisters who were to be sent from Rangoon. To this house which was not found sufficiently roomy, he added another brick building with an upper story which afforded an ample accommodation for the Sisters and their pupils whilst the former building continued to be used as a sleeping room for boarders, a refectory, and other purposes. Two Sisters of the order of St. Joseph of the Apparition went in 1886, and began a school which has been as well attended as it could be in a place like Mandalay. At the same time they assumed charge of the girls orphanage. They were assisted in their work, in the subsequent year, by two other European Sisters and two native novices. The King had promised to send to that School, a number of girls from the palace; but he has not hitherto carried his intentions into execution. He had likewise assured the writer that he would assist the Sisters with money; but with the [illegible]ption of a small sum he gave to them in the beginning, [illegible]ft them to their own very limited resources. Woe to those wh[illegible] their confidence in Princes ! !

New Church at Monhla.

The Fathers Oblats had erected a fine and [illegible]corated brick church in the village of Monhla, but owing to the softness of the ground on which rested the foundations, and also to the frequent earthquakes in that part of Burma, the building began soon to show unmistakeable signs of an approaching danger. Immense cracks in the walls yearly increasing, the Pastor of the place, father D'Isola jointly with the Bishop who visited the place in 1869, resolved not to hold any longer divine service in that locality. It was resolved to pull down the building; in the meanwhile, divine service was performed in a part of the missionary's house. Fortunately, it was easy to procure at a very low price, from a Greek merchant, almost on the spot, all the teak timber that was required. The good Priest set immediately at work, and with the sum of one thousand rupees, given by the Bishop, he was enabled to erect a fine and strongly built church that will last for many years to come.

In 1867, His Majesty the King placed under the charge of Father Lecomte, twelve or fourteen boys belonging to some Officers of his Palace. The boys were to learn the English language, and the rudiments of those sciences that are taught in ordinary European schools. The excellent father has devoted himself to that task with great zeal and courage, and has succeeded as well it was possible to do, with boys of this country.

In each village of the upper country, where is a church, the mission keeps up schools both for the instruction of boys and girls. These schools are, as a matter of course, under the management of Christian native masters and mistresses. Those

Schools are opened to much improvement, but it must be confessed that despite the low standard of the studies, they are the means of doing much good. The children of both sexes learn to read and write; they are taught the christian prayers, as well as a sound knowledge of religion. They acquire a certain mode of demeaning themselves, which counteracts to a certain degree, the tendency to a wild life, which the races of the Mongolian type have such decided a proneness to. There are no people so fond of individual independence, as the Burmans are. It is true they bend their heads under the iron grasp of their heartless rulers, but they lift it up, the very moment that the pressure is no longer immediately felt.

Reflection on the *kalapiets*.

Whilst engaged in writing a few particulars respecting the Mission of Upper Burma, I intend to consign here remarks that I have made on one occasion, when I visited the Christian villages west of the great river Irrawaddy, respecting the *kalapiets* or Christians who at a period more or less remote, and under peculiar circumstances, have apostatized from Christian religion. It is a remarkable fact that many of those individuals whose ancestors have seceded from the faith, more than a century ago, have hardly embraced the Budhist religion. They are, we may say, individuals destitute of all religious principles and yet by a strange anomaly they are more prejudiced against Christian religion than the very Pagans themselves. Their obstinacy and stubborness can scarcely be understood by those who have not seen them. Some among them from mere imitation of the Burmese customs, appear to imitate certain external religious practices, but the greatest number are neither Christians nor Budhists. They are noted for their lawless life, and their irregular behaviour. A Burmese Governor stated to the writer that they were the worst men he had ever come in contact with.

Let us endeavour to fix with a certain degree of exactness the probable epoch when the ancestors of the Kalapiets, have in different places, begun to abandon Christian religion and subsequently fallen in the sad state in which we see them at present. No doubt the desertion has not been sudden; it has been gradually brought in, by various causes, which we do not know with precision but which we can with tolerable probability guess at.

Kalapiets at Khiaungoo.

1. The Kalapiets met with in or about the large village of Khiaungoo are at least, since about 130 years in that state. Upon this point there is not a shadow of doubt. The testimony of the oldest Christians is both unanimous and precise. The Christians who settled in the above named village, came from a place called Yatana.

Letpangyee.

2. In the village of Letpangyee, south west of Monhla, there are about fifteen families of decendants of apostates. The first Christians of that locality were emigrants from the village of Khiansarua: they came thither about 120 years ago, with the probable intention of finding better lands for cultivation, than those of their former residence. Those emigrants have not at once become apostates, since there was among them a small chapel for divine service about 50 or 60 years ago. But owing to the paucity of the missionaries in the upper country, the visits of the priests to the Christian villages were rare and at great intervals. The poor Christians living among the Pagans almost lost in the middle of a pagan centre, intermarrying with pagan Burmese women, left almost destitute of religious instruction, soon followed the customs, manners and habits of the heathens, sent their children into the Burmese monasteries and after the lapse of one generation found themselves almost entirely burmanized, and gradually conformed entirely to the outward budhist practices of their neighbours. In the year 1867, there was but one family that had retained the faith of their ancestors.

Pataong and Kiun-dau

In the two villages of Pataong and Kiundau the number of christians has never been considerable In the latter village, the writer has seen the ground where upon stood a very small chapel and a place for the residence of the priests, when he came to that place. There is no doubt but the number of christians must have been very small, and almost insignificant. The grave of the Priest who died there, is still visible as well as the remnant of the wall that enclosed the burial place. He does not think it was more than 25 feet by 30. The name of the Barnabite Missionary who died there, is Antonio Re. The writer when he visited that place, knelt down in the centre of the small burial place, and with a strong emotion, uttered a prayer for the repose of the souls of the departed faithful whose mortal remains were entombed in that place, and in particular for the worthy Antonio Re. It was on or about the year 1810, under the reign of King Bodaw that the two small congregations were dispersed, owing to a two fold cause, a famine prevailing at that time, and the disordered state of the district, over run by robbers, who not satisfied with pillaging and killing, set fire to all the villages. Moreover those Christian villages having but a small number of families, had not humanely speaking, the elements necessary for maintaining their own life, and support themselves, independent of their numerous neighbours, the Burmans.

Khiaungio.

Close to the small village of Khiaungio, there is a village of Kalapiets, with about 12 houses. From the information that the writer gathered on the spot, it is certain that the inhabitants are in that state, since a remote period, not less than 130 years. What a strange contrast. The small village of Khiaungio is all Christian, whilst the other not more than few miles distant, is peopled by Kalapiets, of the worst description; and most stubborn in their anti-christian dispositions. The writer addressed them with great mildness, inviting them to come to the church, and join anew with the Christians, but it was in vain, and without the least good result. Of course they appeared pleased with what he said to them but it was merely to please him. Their hearts remained as hard as a rock.

List of christians and Kalapiets, under King Bodaw.

Here is a curious list of the number of Christians and also of Kalapiets houses, made under the reign of King Bo-daw about 95 years ago in the year of the Burmese era 1138. It will show the changes that have taken place since that period up to the present time. This list was made chiefly in view of the military service as all christians belong to it. The name of the village of Pareima, on the banks of the Khyin-douin river, is not mentioned. It is asserted, however, it is the place where christians settled on their first arrival in Upper Burmah. There are in a field, some heaps of bricks, which, up to this day, the natives call the place where stood the church of the foreigners, but it is probable that they all migrated to the localities where dwell now their descendants long before the epoch the list was made. There are no villages of Kalapiets in that or the neighbouring places.

There were in 1138:—			There are now 1867:—
at Nabeck houses	... 25	" " "	25
" Khiansarua "	... 55	" " "	105
" Khiangio "	... 24	" " "	25
" Lekpangyee "	... 15	" " "	4
Khet-thin, one christian named Tomè	... 18	" " "	0
Pogniat, South of Ava	... 2	" " "	0
Ye gian, near Khetthin	... 1	" " "	0
Khiaungoo or Tsabaiauk	37	" " "	40
Nagabo	... 17	" " "	2
Tsain piyn	... 16	" " "	0
Khiun dau, Eindaing	... 20	" " "	3
Padouing	... 12	" " "	0
" Tabarin mio " " "	... 18	" " "	3
" Monhla " " "	... 48	" " "	64

Supposing the said list to be a correct one, the inference to be drawn from the above figures is that there are fewer families at present than there were 90 years ago, and that the few families to be found, at that period in several localities, have completely disappeared. The causes that have acted in bringing about this sad result have already been alluded to. The principal one is certainly the penury of Missionaries in the Upper Country during a period of at least forty years. Whoever knows the character and disposition of native Christians, their innate indolence, the weakness of their intellect, their ignorance, their indifference about everything that has not a reference to immediate wants of this life, will readily understand that unless a Priest be incessantly teaching, correcting and encouraging them, they will soon lapse into a state of indifference, ignorance and carelessness concerning religion. During the last 35 years, the congregation of Upper Burma, have not been neglected. The fathers Oblats did everything that could be done in taking care of them. And up to our days, some of the same fathers together with French fathers have laboured in that somewhat unyieiding field with an admirable zeal and praiseworthy self-denial. All their efforts have done little more than keeping up the number of Christians. This however, is a great deal. The military service is the cause of the destruction of many heads of families, particularly when people have to go into the Shan States, to crush certain chronic revolts. If the Priest had not been in the villages to assist, comfort and direct the inhabitants, the writer firmly believes that all vestiges of Christianity would have long ago disappeared, or at least, dwindled into an insignificant number.

Remarks on the present King of Burma.

It is well also to consign in these pages a fact which does honour to the King of Burmah. Since his accession to the throne, in 1852, the reigning sovereign has shewn a real disposition in assisting the missionary residing in the royal city. Father Abbona had known him well, before his accession to the throne. He was then fond of religious studies and had made considerable progress in the science of Budhism. He was fond of conversations on religion, and appeared much pleased with hearing particulars concerning the creed of the foreigners, that is to say, the Catholics. But this fondness was with him, as with all Burmans, the offspring of mere curiosity, and that even, of a very superficial character. Before his Majesty's mind was so much taken up with mercantile speculations, the writer has had often the opportunity of discussing religious topics with him, but he soon found out that the King looked upon such discussions as matters of amusement, intended, at the most, to make a display of his knowledge of the Budhist books, and particularly the metaphysical part of them. Never has he exhibited the least inclination to reflect, even for a moment upon the capital and fundamental truths so peculiar to every rational being, viz., God, the creation, Providence etc., etc. With a childish sneer, he laughed at the idea of a creating power. Now that his mind is entirely engrossed with the gains and profits he is aiming at making, he cares no longer for religious topics, It may be, too, that he has found it impossible to maintain his footing in carrying on a fair discussion, and that he has given it up in despair. Certain it is, that notwithstanding what has been asserted to the contrary by persons who ought to have known better, the King has never had the remotest idea of studying carefully and seriously the tenets of Christianity, and that he has always been a staunch and fervent supporter of Buddhism. He sometimes affects the air of a free-thinker, but his acts belie his language. No King, among his predecessors, has ever displayed a zeal and a liberalty equal to his, in the way of building pagodas, monasteries, shewing respect to the Talapoins, feeding them, and in every way doing honor to them. Is he led in this line of conduct by political views? Does he hope thereby to obtain a greater and stronger influence over the minds of his subjects? I believe that his acute and cunning mind can easily reach so far, and make religion a cloak to cover his views, and a means to carry out his plans.

Be that as it may, it is certain that he has been liberal, in assisting the Mission of Upper Burma. Since his accession to the throne, he gave a monthly aid to Rev. P. Abbona. That aid was, at first, very small, but he has increased it subsequently. Though, owing to certain changes in the royal mind, the aid was not granted for some months, yet the withdrawal was but a temporary one. When the city was transferred from Amerapoora to the present site of Mandalay, the King gave a fine piece of land both for the Church and the dwelling of the Missionary, and bore almost all the expense of building the house. He also contributed towards the erection of the Church. When the Bishop has come to visit the Mission, the King has liberally given him money to defray his travelling expenses, and supplied him with elephants when he had to travel by land, and boats when he had to go by the river. He likewise gave him a few fine pieces of timber for rebuilding the tower of the Church of Rangoon. When some missionaries came for the benefit of their health to the royal city, His majesty always gave them a sum of money for defraying the expense of the voyage.

10

Kindness of the King to Bishop extended to others.

The writer is delighted to consign herein, in a few lines the many tokens of kindness which the King Mindon has bestowed upon the Catholic Mission. But at the same time, to avoid misgivings, it ought to be stated that the liberality of the King extends also to the ministers of other denominations, though to different degrees. The Armenian Priest has a share in the King's bounty, as well as the Chinese monks. He has lately contributed most liberally in setting up a school and a Church for an English minister, belonging to the protestant association for the propagation of the Gospel. It is true that the said minister was backed by the powerful and active influence of the Chief Commissioner of British Burma, as well as by the incessant interference of the English resident at the Court of Mandalay. The King as a true and clever politician, never does any favor without expecting some return in one way or in another. By favoring the English minister, he expects to ingratiate himself in the favor of the English Governor, and hopes to find in his Protege, an individual, who in case of difficulties arising, will be able to lend him, an important support. Moreover the King, in the kindnesses that he vouchsafes to foreign ministers of religion, is influenced, to a great extent, by a thirst of an ill disguised vanity and a strong love of having his name honorably mentioned *et late et circum*, with praises and acclámations for his incomparable generosity.

The crown prince.

In connection with the history of this mission, it is proper to mention one for whom the writer has had always a strong and well merited affection. He has rendered also a good service to the mission. Here allusion is made to the late prince known among the English as the War Prince, the brother to the King and the Heir apparent, who was basely and cowardly assassinated in the month of August 1866, by a handful of comspirators, headed by two sons of the King, his nephews and one of the two, was his son-in-law. He was a man of strong and firm will, bent upon attaining a great object, the civilization of Burma by the means of the knowledge of the sciences and arts of Europe. For that purpose he had sent young men to France, and to India to be educated. They were afterwards to return to their country, importing therein the knowledge they had acquired in foreign countries. In his palace, he had 60 or 70 boys and young men, who after their daily work, spent their evening in studies. He was not himself a learned man, but he had an intuitive instinct to discover that his people wanted knowledge to be enabled to raise themselves in the scale of improvement. His solicitude extended to the women. He entrusted to the writer, four little girls, which were placed by him in the Rangoon Convent, to be educated as European girls of their age. This happened in the year 1863. Those children remained under the management of the Sisters during five years. The Prince, until his death, evinced for them the utmost solicitude not only by paying regularly their board, but also by sending to them presents. After his death, the King continued to pay, for their maintenance during two years. But devoid of his Brother's zeal for promoting education, he recalled them to Mandalay. One of them would not obey the royal summons and is up to this day, in the convent. The good prince during the four last years of his life, gave to the writer the greatest tokens of the warmest affection, accompanied with substantial proofs of his liberality. Had he lived, it is probable that, owing to his good dispostions, Christian religion would have made fair progress among the Burmese. It may truely he said of him, that he has been the last of the Burmans. He will have no successor worthy of him. After the demise of the present ruler, events will prove the truth of the above assertion. It has been much discussed among foreigners at the time that the bloody tragedy was enacted, whether the King had done anything to bring it about, or in other terms whether he had countenanced it directly or indirectly. In the writer's mind, there is not a shadow of doubt on this subject. The King was a stranger to the massacre that had taken place. When the thing was done, and the King being anew firmly seated on his throne, it is probable that he was not sorry to be left alone, undisputed master of his country, and free from all restraint. But, it would be a slander to assert that he connived in any direct or indirect way at the destruction of a brother, who always and on all occasions, showed himself a most obedient subject and loving brother. Moreover the many dangers the King was exposed to, during the time that the bloody tragedy was enacted, shows evidently that the conspirators aimed not only at the ruin of their uncle, but also at seizing if possible the throne, after having destroyed its occupant. They were foiled in their attempt by their own want of energy and foresight ; they acted as a party of drunken dacoits without any well concerted plan. They miserably failed, and were ultimately compelled to run, for saving their lives, into the English territory. Of the two Sons of the King who were the ringleaders of the rebellion, the eldest, the Myin Goon Prince is a prisoner in the fort of Chunar, for misbehavior in Rangoon, the youngest is in Bengal, where he lives, on the bounty of the English Government. The latter was for some time placed under the charge of the writer, by the Chief Commissioner of Pegu, Sir A Phayre, but his successor has, by a series of unjustifiable proceedings, taken him a way from the quiet and safe place he much enjoyed, and sent him almost, as a criminal to the Andamans penal Settlement ; The Supreme Government, however, more just than their Proconsul, have called him to Bengal where he is properly looked after, and his wants are liberally supplied. We cannot penetrate in the bosom of futurity. But in the case of disorders arising after the King's death, it is not, out of the range of probability to suppose that he may be, on account of the education that he is receiving, fixed upon as the fittest person to occupy the throne.

Tragical and of the amiable Padene Prince.

Out of respect for the memory of the late Heir Apparent the King's Brother, let a mention be made of the sad fate that has finally over taken, his amiable eldest Son, the Padein Min. He was dear to the writer both on account to his father and of his own personal merit. During the rebellion of the two King's Sons, in 1866, the Padein Min, found himself in a difficult and most dangerous position. With good reason, he was afraid to fall a victim to the Assassins of his father. He left the royal city in haste crossed the Irrawaddy, and went in the Province of Shoay Bo where his late father had numerous partizans. He soon saw himself at the Head of a respectable army as far as number is concerned, but his followers were ill provided with arms. Instead of remaining on the defensive to protect himself and his family, he became the tool of a few ambitious man who, for promoting their own interests compelled him to carry on war against his uncle the King. He had the best chance of success ; but owing to his timidity and want of experience, he did not improve his position and in a short time, his followers were dispersed and himself made a prisoner. The King at first, spared his life, and put him in strict confinement with iron at his feet, within the palace's enclosure. He remained in this state ;with two of his brothers, for two or three months. The writer went by the order of the King to visit him in prison and assure him of his pardon, and of his majesty's intention to put him soon in a better and more comfortable place. But not long after this interview, the people of Rangoon heard with horror, that the unfortunate Prince had been put to death, despite the effort of the English Agent to save his life. It seems probable that the King urged on by the Queen, who hated the young and amiable Prince, gave relectantly the order of his execution. The writer was painfully affected by this sad news as he well recollected the touching words by which his father had on one occasion, recommended his Son to his care and protection.

CONTINUATION OF THE OUTLINE OF THE HISTORY OF THE MISSION DOWN TO THE YEAR 1877.

I will continue to mention a few particulars regarding the Upper Burma Mission until its separation from the Mission of lower Burma in 1871, but completed or effected in January 1873. After the death of the Crown Prince, and the almost total destruction of his family, followed by the revolt of two of his sons, the King grew fearful and timorous. He thought his position beset with perils and dangers. Thence his settled idea of concentrating all the power in his hands. Contrary to the custom previaling from immemorial time of having always a Member of the royal family appointed Heir apparent with suitable amount of power, influence and courtly retinue the King would never allow one of his sons to be raised to that dignity. He feared lest he might plot against him, and with the forces in his hands, hurl him from the throne. The head of the Budhist religion called *Thathana paing* happened to die two years after the Heir apparent ; the King would not suffer another to be promoted in his stead. He told the writer in the course of one conversation, that he himself assisted by four dignitaries would manage all matters of a religious character. He is a true Czar in his Dominions. His greed of influence and power is so great that he wishes to be the only trader in his Dominions, and the only man who has a right to grasp profits. But withal he is not a miser. He is fond of money not for the sake of hoarding it as his predecessors did he wished to have money but for spending it as he liked.

His majesty did all in his power to induce the writer to fix his residence in the capital. He promised him a monthly allowance for personal support. He gave him a very fine and extensive piece of ground whereupon a spacious brick building was erected for his residence. The writer expressed to the King his grateful acknowledgements for this act of kindness. He took possession of the place, but never dwelt therein. He devoted the building for a School, and up to this day it is used for that purpose.

During the absence of the Vicar apostolic, the Mission of Upper Burma was administered by a Provicar apostolic, the very Rev. Father Abbona. But on account of the great distance that separated the various parts of the extensive Mission of Ava and Pegu, the Vicar apostolic had resolved to have it divided, if possible, into three parts. British Burmah, with the Province of Arracan in the South, Burma proper in the North, and Toungoo with the Country on the East, and stretching on the North, as far as the Southern boundaries of China. In 1869, the Vicar apostolic, went to Europe for the purpose of sitting at the General Council that was to be opened in November of the same year in the Vatican. He availed himself of his stay in Rome in order to have the above related division carried into execution by the Authority of the Congregation de Propaganda Fide. Everything was arranged agreeably to the particular's that were suggested. One of the Secretaries of the Propaganda, named Mgr. Jacobini, a man remarkably intelligent and well informed, was the person who was charged by the Cardinal prefect to study the subject, and draw a report, to be hereafter submitted to the Board of the Congregation. The writer had several interviews with Mgr. Jacobini, within the apartments of the Propaganda, and in his own logdings in which the question was seriously discussed. The result was the partition of the Mission, as above mentioned. The Mission of British Burma was called Missio Birmaniæ Meridionalis—the Mission in the North, comprising Burma Proper and stretching to the Southern boundaries of Yunan was designated : Missio Birmaniæ Septen trionalis ; the third division comprised the town of Tounghoo, and all the territories, east of that city, as far as the Salween and Mekon river, and stretching in the North, to the Southern boundaries of China. This part received the appellation of Missio Birmaniæ Orientalis.

The Mission of Southern Burma was assigned to the writer of these lines. When in Rome, Cardinal Barnabo told him, that being as yet the Coadjutor of the Malayan Mission, *cum titulo successionis*, and Bishop Boucho being old and requesting the aid of his Coadjutor for carrying on the administration of the mission, he gave him full liberty to make choice either to go to Malesia, or to remain in Burma. He begged a few days to consider seriously on a subject of so much importance. When he had before God made up his mind, he went to his Eminence's apartments, and stated that, though he felt a strong affection for the Malayan Mission, where he had laboured for fourteen years, yet he felt that it was his duty to remain in Burma, where his presence was more wanted, and an ampler field of labour was open before him. He therefore begged to be allowed to continue to carry on the administration of the Mission of Burma. The Cardinal said that he was delighted at such a choice being made, and added that he sanctioned it with his whole heart.

In the year 1872, the Bull appointing the Rev. A. Bourdon, apostolic Missionary in Burma, residing at Rangoon for the last eight years, Bishop of Dardania *in partibus infidelium*, and Vicar apostolic of Northern Burma, was received at Rangoon. No better choice could have been made. The Bishop was as yet young, talented, zealous and eminently fitted for fulfilling the arduous duties of his new position. On the 5th of January of the following year, he was consecrated by the writer, in the Church of Rangoon, in the presence of all the Clergy of the Mission, of all the Chief Authorities of the place, and of all the Congregation. Such a splendid and edifying sight had never been witnessed in the City of Rangoon.

A few days afterwards, the new Bishop left Rangoon, to go and take possession of his new field of labour. The writer accompanied him to the Capital and introduced him to his new flock. This business being over, he bade a final farewell to all those who had been committed to his care during a period of nearly fifteen years, and returned to Rangoon. Here must end this notice regarding the Mission of Northern Burma, since it has been placed under the direction of a new, able and zealous Chief Pastor.

The Mission of eastern Burma remained connected with the Southern Burma Mission, until the year 1867. At that time the sacred Congregation had been urgently requested several times, to allow the important territory east of Tounghoo, to be placed in the hands of a Society that could assume charge of it. The request was at last granted. The new Society of foreign Missions recently established at Milan, was requested to assume charge of the New Mission. In the above mentioned year, the very Rev. E. Biffi arrived from Italy with four fellow-labourers. After a stay of 15 days at Rangoon, he proceeded with his companions to Toungoo, where he has been staying and endeavouring to establish a Mission among the Karens living on the Hills. The zealous efforts of those worthy propagators of vivifying faith, has been rewarded with considerable success. It is to be hoped that they will ultimately succeed in obtaining a firm footing among the Karens, who dwell on a fine and healthy plateau, that stretches very far in the North. They are known under the appellation of Karennee, or Red Karens.

Though the Eastern Burma Mission was begun several years before 1870, it was only at that period that it was officially erected into an apostolic Prefecture, and its limits definitely fixed. As a matter, of course, we have not to occupy ourselves any more concerning a Mission that has passed into other hands. We have to busy ourselves about the Southern Burma Mission, and mention the chief particulars of interest concerning its various localities.

THE SOUTHERN BURMA MISSION.

Before proceeding on with this work, I will here mention the names of all the Missionaries that have arrived in the Mission from the year 1863 to the present year 1877. This will enable the reader to recognize them well, as they may happen to be mentioned by name in the course of the narrative of the particulars that have occurred in this Mission.

Rev. J. B. Bringaud came in the Mission in ...	1863
„ S. Schmitt, ...	1865
„ H. Baert, ...	1869
„ J. Zahm, ...	1869
„ I. L. Rouvreur,...	1870
„ L. C. Petit, ...	1872
„ J. M. T. Cherbonnier, ...	1873
„ R. Cartreau, ...	1873
„ J. Gandon, ...	1874
„ G. Kern, ...	1875
„ N. P. Sadoux	1877
„ Ch. Rouyer	1877

Mergui, Tavoy, Kadai.

Let us begin the continuation of our narrative, with the Southernmost parts of the Mission. There are only two places of some importance, Mergui and Tavoy. The former town situated on the Delta of the River Tenasserim, contains hardly 200 Christians. The number was more considerable some 35 years ago, but it has decreased of at least one third of the total, by emigration to the more prosperous and flourishing cities of Maulmein and Rangoon. Tavoy situated inland, on the river of that name, at a distance of nearly 30 miles from the sea, has a Catholic population of 80 or 90 souls. It is nearly the same number that there was 40 years ago. It would have certainly increased, had not the same cause above mentioned with regard to Mergui, operated also at Tavoy, to a degree proportionate to the number of the Christian population. Between Tavoy and Mergui, but nearer to the latter place, there is a small river called the Kaday river. At its head water, there is a small community of Karens, numbering about 50 souls. Such is the actual state of the small congregations in those three localities.

Death of the Rev. J. Renier.

The Rev. Joseph Renier, has been more than 30 years in spiritual charge of those Congregations. He resided chiefly at Mergui, and visited occasionally the stations of Tavoy and Kaday. Attacked with a serious illness, he came to Maulmain for the purpose of receiving the benefit of a regular medical attendance. But all was of no avail. After a prolonged illness, he felt that his last hour had at last come. He meekly resigned his soul into the hands of his Maker and expired in January of the year 1872.

Rebuilding of the Church and Presbytery at Mergui.

It was during his ministration, that Mr. George de Castro rebuilt at his own expense, first the house of the Priest, and next, the Church that had been consumed during the conflagration that destroyed the greatest part of the town, in the beginning of 1856, and thereby doubly entitled himself to the honorable title of Kiaongtaga.

Church of Tavoy.

His eldest son Mr. Domingo D'Castro treading upon the footsteps of his worthy father, has entitled himself to a similar distinction, by rebuilding the church at Tavoy, supplying it with all the necessary furnitures and finally building a very substantial house for the use of the Priest, when he visits Tavoy. It is hardly possible to exceed in praising the conduct of that worthy man, who, not satisfied with his liberalities, acts as a fervent Catechist during the absence of the Priest. After the demise of Father Renier, the Rev. J. Zahm visited from Maulmain once a year at least, the three small Congregations.

Rev. Cherbonnier in charge.

In the year 1874, Rev. Father Cherbonnier went to take charge permanently of these stations. His principal residence is at Mergui. He visits frequently Tavoy and Kaday.

Maulmain building of the Church at Mayangon.

In the town of Maulmain there are two distinct Churches, the one at Mayangon, St. Mary's, and the other principal one, St. Patrick's. In Mayangon there was a good wooden Church, to which were attached several rooms, used for the residence of the Clergyman in that locality. The part of the building used for the Church was in many respects insufficient for the increasing Congregation. In 1865, the Rev. Father Chevillon, thought of building for himself a house separated from the Church and afford thereby an increase to the church by pulling down the partition that separated the rooms occupied as a residence by the Clergyman, and thereby allowing a considerable space for the enlarging of the church. The house was at first erected at the East of this Church; subsequently pulled down and rebuilt, on the West side, nearer to the road, on the spot where it stands to this day. This measure proved for a time satisfactory to the Congregation. But soon after they were not pleased with this new arrangement. They saw St. Patrick's Church to be a fine and substantial brick building. They wished to have also for themselves a building of a similar appearance, and of an equally substantial nature. All the members of the Congregation, united as a man, came forward to offer their contributions, each according to his own means. A capital of several thousand Rupees, being obtained, the Rev. Father Zahm, pastor of the place, thought that the moment had come for laying down the foundations. This was done in the year 1869, and in the course of the following year, it was completed so far, as to be fitted for the celebration of divine service. Subsequently a belfry was added, giving a fine appearance to the Church. The interior has been well arranged, disposed and decorated by the indefatigable exertions of Father Zahm. Among the benefactors of the new Church, the writer must record the name of Mrs. Joanna Gomez, who alone has contributed more than 4000 Rupees, and that of Mr. Raymund, who has also shown a most praiseworthy generosity.

Erection of the Girls' School.

In 1865, a Girls' School was erected South of the Church, at the expense of Mrs. Regina Amisitta, mother-in law to M. Boniface Boudville. The building lasted ten years. It then required repairs. Father Zahm thought that it was better to pull down the building, and, with the serviceable materials and the addition of new ones, to erect a larger building, intended not only for a School, but designed to be also a reading Club and a place of rendezvous for young men, to spend agreeably and profitably their evenings. The building was begun in 1875, and completed in the following year. It is lofty, well ventilated and thoroughly well adapted for the several purposes intended by its projector. The school is vast and capable of accommodating more than 130 pupils. The other part, intended for the various purposes already mentioned, is entirely separated from the School by a strong partition. Each department is reached by a separate staircase.

St. Patrick's Church.

At St. Patrick's Church, great improvements have taken place during the period that is now under review. The old convent built in the year 1844 and 1845 with good teak materials, offered many signs of decay, seventeen years after its erection. To repair it in a substantial manner, would have required a very large outlay of money. Suc hrepairs could not even have preserved the building for a long time. Moreover, the Convent, as it was, could not afford a sufficient room for the increasing number of pupils. The Rev. Father Ducotey, who was as yet in spiritual charge of Maulmain, resolved to undertake the construction of a new Convent in bricks. A building in bricks demanded a large outlay of money. However with the assistance he received from the inhabitants of Maulmain, he bravely set at work. The materials he got from the old house, availed him much for carrying out the great work. The writer contributed a sum of

Re-building of the Convent.

Rupees 4,000 towards the completion of the building. It was in the year 1863, that the sisters with their pupils removed into the new premises. A little while after, the Rev. X. Ducotey, left Maulmain and was succeeded by the Rev. Father Guerin. In the year 1867, a broad portico was added to the Convent, which afforded to the Sisters, a very commodious room for the performance of their daily spiritual devotions, and for a place of daily meeting.

In the year 1873, the Southern wing, too small for the large number of boarders, was considerably extended, affording in the lower story, additional rooms for Schools, and in the upper one, more extensive dormitories and a fine dressing room. I ought to have mentioned also, that in 1867, a good wooden building, with a tiled roof was erected close to the main building, for a refectory for the use of both Sisters and boarders. In the year 1875, a strong and high wall was erected to protect the extensive boundary of the burying ground.

In the year 1876, a light but elegant portico was raised in front of the St Patrick's Church, on the plan supplied by Rev. Father Zahm, and at the sole expense of Dr. Slym. The Rev. Father Guerin was also endeavouring to find resources for rebuilding the present Boys School, on a site both beautiful and extensive.

Amherst.

At the mouth of the Salween, on the left bank, there is a large village, called by the Natives, Kiaikamee, and Amherst, by the English in honour of Lord Amherst, who was Governor General of India, when the place was taken possession of, in 1824. It has always been a station for the Pilots, who have to take ships up to Maulmain. In 1851, three Catholic Pilots purchased at their own expense, a ground and house from a certain Captain Lea, for the purpose of converting the house into a place of Worship. A house was subsequently erected for the use of the Priest when he visits the station. The above mentioned ground and house were regularly made over by the three parties, to the Mission, in the person of Dr. Balma, the then Vicar apostolic. The deed is probably still existing in the Church of Maulmain. The place is visited two or three times a year, by one of the clergyman residing in that town.

Brohter's School at Rangoon.

During the period under review, the cause of education has been vigorously promoted throughout the Mission, and particularly in Rangoon. The locality near the Church, which was occupied by the Christian Brothers, was in the opinion of the writer no longer suited as an Institution. It had become by far too small for the ever increasing number of pupils. The Head of the Mission was fortunate enough in securing by purchase, the possession of a fine roomy house with an extensive compound, situated in the centre of the town, close to the Soolay Pagoda, and in the vicinity of the Church. All the necessary arrangements having been made for securing large and airy school rooms, and extensive out-offices, the Christian Brothers took possession of the new premises in the year 1867. The total cost of the building, including all the improvements that have been made is Rupees 28,000. The English Government had the generosity to give, as a School building grant, one half of the above mentioned sum. A brick building, intended for the accommodation of boarders, has been subsequently erected at the expense of the Brothers. The School has always been very flourishing, and gives general satisfaction.

New Convent at Rangoon.

The English boarding and day School for Girls, in Fraser Street, had passed into the hands of the Sisters of the Good Shepherd in the year 1867. The Sisters of St. Joseph, who had hitherto been in charge of it, were sent to Mandalay, to take possession of the New Convent erected in that Capital. The Convent in Fraser Street, soon proved too small for the daily increasing pupils. Moreover the quarter in which it is situated, was at first, airy and pleasant, but all the vacant lots that were then unoccupied, became soon covered with buildings, which gradually surrounded as it were, the Convent in every direction. It was of an absolute necessity, to look out for a spot better suited for a School and a Convent, and for erecting threreon a building suitable for both purposes. The Superior of the Mission fixed his choice upon a fine piece of land, in Commissioner's road, west of " Phayre Lodge," containing 5 acres and a half. On the North, it is limited by the railway line and the military parade ground, and on the South by a

100 feet road and the public garden. The land was purchased in the year 1872. In the following year, with a stout heart and an immense trust in Providence, the writer began to lay the foundations of the splendid building which at last has been finished and supplied with the full complement of out-offices. All the ground is now surrounded with a wall seven feet high, from the surface of the soil. The total expense for the purchase of the land, the erection of the buildings, and the immense wall that encircles the ground, is Rupees 85,000. The Government has allowed a grant-in-aid on three occasions, amounting to 19,000 Rupees. The work of the Ste Enfance, during four years has allowed an aggregate sum of nearly 20,000 Rupees. From various other sources, including the benefit accrued from a sum of Rupees 30,000, lent by the local Government for three years without interests, about Rupees 19,000, all together 58,000 Rupees. The remaining 27,000 have been paid by the head of the Mission, from his own private resources.

The building of the Old Convent, together with that of the Orphanage, is reserved for the sole use of the Orphans, whose number is fast increasing. In addition to the Burmese Orphans School, the Sisters keep a separate English day School, for the benefit of the children of poor parents, who have no means to send their girls to the new Convent.

New Church of St. John.

In the year 1877, on a spot of land, north of the old Convent compound, where formerly had stood a Chapel, there has been erected a good substantial brick Church of an octagonal shape. It is dedicated to God, under the invocation of St. John the Baptist, the patron Saint of that locality for the last hundred and thirty years. That Church is intended for the use of the Orphans, and of all the Christians using the Burmese language. It was intended as a place of worship, where instruction shall be given only in the vernacular language. It is but right that in a town like Rangoon, there should be a place of worship appropriated for the use of the Burmese speaking population. It will form the link of connection, between the Christians and the Burmese. It is the more necessary to have such a place, that the Burmese are but too prone to look upon the Christian religion, as that of foreigners, and not as a religion that is intended for all persons, irrespective of their nationalities.

The Church in cantonment had its tower completed in 1870 at the expense of Government. Since the Rev. Father LeRouvreur was in charge of the Tamil Congregation, a great improvement had taken place.

St Anthony's Church.

It was then found out that their number exceeded all that was anticipated. As a temporary measure, the small Chapel that was erected on a piece of land adjacent to the ground of the Old Convent, was used for divine service. It was overcrowded every Sunday. The Head of the Mission exerted himself much for securing the possession of a favourable site for erecting a Church and a School for the benefit of the Tamil congregation and of their numerous offsprings. At last, after great exertions and some disappointment, the Honourable Ashley Eden, then Chief Commissioner of British Burma, consented to let the Head of the Mission have a fine spot of land on the East side of Phayre Street, opposite the small lake. Being offered by the writer the upset price of Government for the conceded ground, he generously refused to take it ; he graciously added that it was a free grant conceded by Government, and ordered that the papers conveying the deed should be forthwith drawn up and handed over to the head of the mission without any expense whatsoever.

No time was lost by the Rev. LeRouvreur. He forthwith took possession of the land, fenced it, and had it cleared from all rubbish, and levelled as much as it could be. The writer believes that it is well to mention, as a subject of edification, the enthusiastic zeal and fervent earnestness which the members of the Tamil congregation have dispayed in assisting their Pastor in the work he had undertaken. A number of sappers and miners devoted all their spare time, to come from a great distance to work for levelling the ground, digging the foundations, and making themselves otherwise useful. Men women and children rivalled with each other in assisting in the good work. How consoling is such an instance of religious fervor ! With some assistance which he received, the Priest built a large and substantial plank house, intended for a School during the week days, and for a place of worship on Sundays and Holy days of obligation. It can accommodate from 400 to 500 souls, as the members of the Congregation do not use seats, but sit on the floor.

Not as yet satisfied with this provisory arrangement, the zealous Pastor thought of erecting upon a rising part of the compound, a good brick Church. The foundations were dug, and the corner stone laid in the year 1874. The work went on slowly for want of means to push it on with rapidity. Every year some addition was made, and at last, in the year 1877, the roof and ceiling were put on, at an expense of Rupees 4,500. Mr. J. Darwood generously came forward to the assistance of the Church, and paid the amount. The doors and windows have been put up and the inside of the walls well plastered. The floor being made of broken bricks connected together by mortar, and lined with cement will soon be finished and the church will be ready for divine service in a short space of time. Of course the belfry and portico are not as yet made, but one can easily afford to wait for these ornamental appendages.

Shaboa Mission.

Rev. Father D. Tarrolly, having left Myaungmya, came to settle in a place called Shaboa, somewhere below the village of Twantay. The reason that induced him to go to such an out of the way place, was that there were few people whom he had known before, who had invited him to come and settle among them. He lived there until the arrival in the Mission, of Father Schmitt, whom the Superior of the Mission had sent to help and assist him. The good Father was not pleased with that measure. On a sudden he left Shaboa and came to settle in the midst of paddy fields, among some Karen families at a place, called Khiaung-wine. He remained there, and also at a place called Konta, where the people gave him a Khiaung or Budhist monastery abandoned by the former inmates. Tired of being alone in those places, he applied for leave to return to Myaungmya, where he is at present doing all what he can for the benefit of his old converts.

Rev. S. Schmitt has laboured much in all the district of Twantay, and in the direction of the sea, towards the south west. He has established several small Chapels, in various localities, where he temporarily dwells and instructs the Christians and Catechumens. The principal ones are at Shaboa, Tseitgye, Natsingon, Pyaubuay, etc.

His missionary exertions are attended with great labour and fatigue. He lives as a Karen, eats as a Karen, and in every respect, with the exception of the dress, has assimilated himself to them. He is fortunately gifted with an iron constitution, which enables him to bear hardships that would kill any one but him. He has made many converts, but as they are dispersed over an extensive tract, it is very difficult to see them often and to communicate to them the required religious instruction and Christian training.

The Deacon, Thomas, brought up in our College at Pinang, is watching over the Native christians at Khiaung Wine, Konta and other little places not far distant. He has been ordained Priest in the month of January 1878.

Thonzeh Station.

In the year 1870, Rev. H. Baert, had been induced to go to a certain locality, called Thonzeh which at that time, was of a very difficult access from Rangoon. Guided by worthless individuals who abused of his inexperience, he baptized about 18 or 20 persons. After a short stay in that place, he returned to Rangoon. Things remained in that state until the year 1873, when Rev. J. Pakin, returning from Mandalay, was sent to Thonzeh with the intention of beginning seriously a Mission at that place. He was well fitted for that work. The Mission was intended for the Burmese principally, and the Burmese language was his mother tongue. He has had some limited success. With time, it is to be hoped that the good work shall be successfully promoted. There is a Chapel to which two rooms for the residence of the Priest are added. Underneath a Boy's School is kept up by the Clericus Andreas, who is Father Pakin's assistant. A quantity of timber is gathered in the compound, for erecting hereafter a better kind of Chapel. Now the access to Thonzeh is easy and cheap, as the Railway passes through the village, and there is a station at the entrance of it.

Station at Talaindat.

In following up from Rangoon the Yandoon creek, about three miles before reaching the populous village of Niaungdon, on the right bank, at a place called Talaindat, a mission has been begun in the year 1874, by Rev. Father Devos, among the Karens living in those localities. Sickness having unexpectedly come over him, he was obliged to leave not only the place, but even the Mission, as there was no hope of a permanent cure of his infirmities. During his stay at Talaindat, he had begun a good plank-house on the bank of the stream, intended as his residence, also a Chapel above, and School below. Father Gandon sueceeded him in 1876. He has completed the Mission house and given thereto a tolerably good appearence. The house is on a healthy spot, and in a compound planted with fruit trees belonging to the Mission. With time, patience and active exertions, in the discharge of missionary duties, a christianity will be established on a considerable scale. The great draw back for establishing a flourishing Church, that could be well looked after and cared for, is the dispersion of the Karens all over the paddy fields, in small groups of three or four houses, and in places almost inapproachable during the rainy season. When will come the time, Karens exchanging their present deeply rooted habits, will find and appreciate the advantage of living in large villages as their neighbonrs, the Burmese, and form large communities? This will be accomplished slowly by the inevitable absorption of the inferior race by the more influential one. Until that is done by the certain course of things, the Karens, it is to be feared will always remain scattered over fields and jungles, pretty much as we see them in the present day.

Kanatzogon.

Under the zealous and active management of the Rev. Father Bertrand, the Station of Kanatzogon has made great and important progress. In point of material improvement, it has taken the lead of all other stations in the field of the Karen Mission. During the space of four or five years, the old buildings have entirely disappeared, and have been replaced by new, handsome and substantial ones. The Church, the two School houses, one for the Boys, another for the Girls, the house for the missionary's residence are constructions which would grace and adorn any place where they would be erected. The Church is built on a solid brick foundation. The roof is supported by broad brick pillars, and the space between them is filled by thick teak planks that form the walling. In the interior, two rows of brick round pillars have a pleasing appearance. The building is a little wonder in the midst of these localities, which are studded only with poor Karen huts. The Girls' School is a large and substantial teak building, having ample accommodation for the School on the ground floor, and the residence of the Mistresses and their pupils on the upper storey. The School is managed and conducted by two native Sisters, who afford the greatest satisfaction both to the Priest and to the Parents. The Boy's School is equally well built and affords ample room both for the studies and the lodging of the Boys. The Priest's house is high, roomy and comfortable. It is worth noticing that those fabrics have been erected almost entirely by the liberal donations of the members of the congregation. The estimated expense cannot possibly be less then 12,000 or 15,000 Rupees. This is a large sum of money contributed by a Congregation of about 1,600 souls, during a period of five years, who have no other resources but the produce of their paddy lands. It is true the lands of the island of Kanatzogon are both extensive and very fertile. They have the advantage of being regularly inundated by the river water which deposits on them a fertilizing sediment, which causes them to produce yearly, without being exhausted, an abundant crop. At a place called Taraumaraik, there is the nucleus of an important Congregation, composed solely of Bama Karens, under the control of an excellent man, named Sabelay, who by his age, his virtues and his superior instruction, has an undisputed superiority over all other christians at that place. He does much good in that locality. In fact, apart from the administration of the Sacraments, he does the duties of a Pastor, and maintains his village in an excellent order. Would to God, the mission possessed in other groups of houses or villages such excellent and zealous headmen! It is the want of properly instructed and zealous chiefs of villages that renders the progress of religion comparatively slow, and the christianizing of the customs and manners of the people, still slower,

During the period under review, the Station of Myaungmya, though labouring under several disadvantages owing to the changes of Pastors and other causes, has not remained stationary, but has also considerably progressed. Father Domingo, after having laboured in several localities of the districts of Dala and Twantay, had at last returned to Myaungmya, which had been the seat of his first labours among the Karen people. He was assisted by Father Devos, whom sickness compelled soon to leave the Mission for a time. He was replaced by Father Cartreau, who has done much for the material and spiritual improvement of the place. Possessed of much zeal and of a robust constitution, he worked with courage and resolution to bring back many Christians, who had almost abandoned the practices of religion, and lived in a state of complete indifference. The Boys' School has been well attended and conducted on sound and excellent principles. The building is rather small and insufficient for the number of Boys that frequent the School. Owing to the fact that the Karens live scattered in the middle of jungle and fields, almost all the boys are boarders, and the result is that extensive premises are required for sheltering 40 boys. The Church and School have received each a good and substantial shingle roof. The Girls' School has been much extended, and is now amply sufficient for any purpose. At the end of 1877, father Cartreau left Myaungmya for a new field not very distant, where a small christian Congregation has been established. There is no doubt but he will succeed with the help of God, in doing much good and founding a flourishing Christian Church among the Karens.

Myoungmya.

Rev. Cartreau.

Rev. Cartreau leaves Myoungmya.

A young Missionary, Rev. Kern is now at Myaungmya, with Father Domingo. The premises for the Boys' School are narrow and insufficient. The missionaries are endeavouring to gather the materials necessary for erecting a suitable building. The church and the Priest's house have received a good shingle roof, which, though expensive at first, is, after all, much cheaper than the ordinary dany-leaves

Rev. G. Kern.

roof. Moreover, it is not so much exposed to the danger of fire.

Great efforts are being made for enlarging the plantation, south of the Church. An attempt is made to plant teak trees, on a spot of ground contiguous to the garden already possessed, which has been granted by Government.

Myaungmya is the first station established by Catholic Missionaries in Pegu, among the Karens. It was begun with great zeal and determination by the Rev. D. Tarolly, then stationed at Bassein, in or about the year 1846. By his admirable perseverance he found himself at the head of a considerable Congregation. He erected a very large and substantial building for a Church, and also with adjacent rooms for his residence. He had also with him a number of Christian boys. Every thing seemed to prosper, the grand work was consolidated and took a progressive development when the breaking out of the war between the English and Burmese, in the year 1852, destroyed in a few days the great work accomplished by the fervent Missionary, at the cost of so much labour and expense. The Burmese, seized with a fit of frenzy, so common with them under circumstances of great excitement, set fire to the mission buildings, beat the people that were guarding the Church, but offered no annoyance to the Christians living in the neighbourhood. The worthy Missionary was arrested, loaded with chains, and in company with Rev. Father Gabutti, was sent up to Ava, as a prisoner. Having reached the Capital, the two prisoners were left at liberty to go and live with their brother Missionaries residing in the Capital. Peace having been concluded in 1853, the zealous Father Domingo, hastened back to his dear station of Myaungmya. With the aid he received from the Mission, and also what he collected, he resolutely set at work to re-build the Church. When the writer visited the place in 1856, he found the present building already standing and complete. The schools for boys and girls were beginning to work on regularly. The Mission in that place has not since, made much progress, owing to several untoward occurrences, and the short time that several Missionaries have been in that locality. Moreover the several groups of Christian houses, are much distant from the Church. Converts cannot receive the amount of care and instruction so much needed by people of a dull understanding. and who have not yet had time to be trained to the practices of religion. It is to be hoped that by means of schools, the boys and girls shall be better instructed and more effectually trained to a Christian life, and will be the means of bringing about a revival in that Christianity which is particularly interesting on account of its being the first, at least, in the province of Bassein. During the period under review, the Missionaries that have laboured in that locality are: Rev. P. Bertrand, who worked there with great zeal, during a period of nearly two years, for repairing the mischief done by his predecessor. Having returned to Kanatzogon he was succeeded by Father Devos, who exerted himself as much as his mental infirmities could allow him. On account of ill-health, he had to leave Myaungmya. He had been assisted by old Father Domingo, during nearly two years. Father Cartreau, who came after him, worked very hard indeed during two or three years. He was directed afterwards to go to set up and revive a new Christianity, North-west of Myaungmya, called Kiuntalok, where his zeal has already infused a new life.

Bassein.

Let us now pass over to Bassein. As there were Christians in the town of Bassein, during a considerable time, previous to the period under review, it is perhaps not uninteresting to state in a few words what is known concerning the small Christian Congregation in that remote part of the province of Pegu. During the latter part of the 16th Century, the whole of the 17th, Portuguese adventurers and merchants made their appearance in these parts, as they did at Dacca, Chittagong, Pegu, and even at Ava.

There is no doubt some of them, and their descendants, settled at Bassein. In the 18th Century, we are informed that some European merchants and navigators were found established in that town, on the bank of the river at the southern extremity. From Rangoon, a Father Barnabite, visited Bassein at least once a year, for the special object of ministering to the spiritual wants of the small Catholic community. Close to a house belonging to Mr. Pilot MacLeod, there is a tank, which formed the limit of a small piece of ground, planted with a few cocoanut trees, upon which was erected an unconsiderable building which was used for divine worship. The writer has seen a remnant of bricks, indicating that the building, if not erected entirely with bricks, had at least, a brick foundation. This state of things lasted until the war that broke out between the English and the Burmese in 1824-25. The house and the small Church belonging to the foreigners, were completely burnt and destroyed, as it is customary with the Burmese in time of war, to do under the barbarous principle: that law sleeps during such calamitous periods. No notice is ever taken of the doings that have taken place during war time. Not long after the war there was at Bassein an Armenian Catholic named Joseph, filling the important post of Collector of Sea Customs or Shabundar of Bassein. In or about the year 1840, Rev. D. Tarolly went from Rangoon to Bassein to visit that station. He thought that the town was admirably situated for the centre of a Missionary establishment, destined to radiate in various directions, among the Karens living in the neighbourhood. Joseph the Armenian, procured for the priest, a good piece of ground in a very quiet and yet a central position. He built on the spot, two good wooden buildings, connected one with the other, as it is usual with the Burmese *Kiaungs* or Monasteries, one for the priest's residence and another for divine service. A small school was kept up in the house of the worthy Missionary. Meanwhile Father Domingo set at work for establishing a Christian Mission in two or three localities of the neighbourhood. Having received a good reinforcement of fellow labourers in the persons of Rev. Jacobo Pogolotti, Vincenti Gabutti, and Candido Paruzza, Father Domingo carried his views a little further. He obtained from the Governor of Bassein the necessary permission to go and establish himself on a healthy, elevated spot near the large village of Myaung mya. We have mentioned in a foregoing article the obstacles he met in his Missionary career at that spot, owing to the second war of 1852.

Father Gabutti at Bassein.

When the writer visited Bassein in 1856 he found the Rev. V. Gabutti in charge of the place. The Christian Community was composed of a certain number of Karens of the neighbourhood, of some inhabitants of Bassein, and of a portion of a detachment of European troops, then stationed at Bassein. On account of ill health, Father Gabutti, was removed to Moulmain. His successor was Rev. R. Naude, who during a stay of about one year, baptized in the jail of Bassein, many of the unfortunate prisoners, arrested under the pretext of having shared in the revolt of what they called the Karen Mengtha. At that time there was at Bassien, a Chapel built with the posts and planks of an old Burmese Monastery, by the exertions of the soldiers then in garrison at that station. Two rooms contiguous to the Chapel, formed the low and humble residence of the Missionary. The Rev. Naude, having left Bassein for the Henzadah district, the Rev. P. Barbe, went to assume temporarily spiritual charge of the place. He erected a house for the Priest, a tolerably good building, in 1857. He remained there about 18 months, when he was succeeded by the Rev. P. Dumollard, who was sent thither for the express purpose of establishing a kind of normal School, for the special object of training up young Karen boys for the duties of teachers and Catechists, and also to prepare a few of them to be sent as students in our College general of Penang, to study the Latin tongue, and be prepared for the ecclesiastical state. Father Dumollard set resolutely at work. In 1860 or 1861, the foundations of the Institution were at first erected with a roomy place for the Printing establishment. He then began the great building of St. Peter's Institution, so named after the Rev. Peter Barbe, who died in 1861, leaving all his property to the Mission, with the exception of a sum of 4,000 Rupees, willed for a special purpose. The remainder of the money amounting to about 12,000 Rupees, was solely and entirely devoted to the erection of the extensive premises. The work was carried on rapidly, and in a way that combined strength with usefulness. I believe that it could have hardly been executed in a manner better suited for the contemplated purpose.

Rev. Naude at Bassein.

Rev. Dumollard at Bassein.

A small community of Christian Brothers was likewise established in that locality, as a Noviciate for all the Schools of the Mission, managed by the Members of the same Society. The Brothers kept at the same time an English day School, attended

Christian Brothers at Bassein.

by about 60 or 70 children from the town.

The Press was sadly in want of English and Burmese types. The former could easily be procured from Calcutta. For the supply of the latter, the Mission was at the mercy of the Baptist's press. The head of the Mission resolved to send to Europe the Rev. P. Dumollard for the express purpose of procuring matrices and puncheons for casting Burmese types in any quantity that might be required. The Rev. gentleman succeeded in having everything done at Paris, in a very creditable manner. On his return, he brought back with him, besides the articles necessary for casting types, about three sets of types cast in Paris.

Press established at Bassein.

During the period of his absence, the post of Bassein was tenanted by the Rev. X. Ducotey. On his return from Europe Father Dumollard applied himself to have the Press in a good working order. In a very short time, the Mission possessed in Burmese a very complete Prayer-Book with the Epistles and Gospels of every Sunday and the principal festivals throughout the year, the books necessary for the Schools, such as Alphabets, treatises of Geography and Arithmetic, the Life of our Lord, and several other works of minor importance. It was in the middle of this useful career, that the Rev. P. Dumollard, owing to some hitherto unexplained misunderstanding, and to the evil and fatal influence exercised over him by a false Brother, took the fatal resolution to leave the mission and return to Europe in 1868. He was succeeded by the Rev. G. D'Cruz, who was eminently fitted for the situation. Under his active and persevering efforts, the institution has made great progress. The number of pupils has much increased, and the Press has been worked with energy. A considerable collection of instructions written by one of the Fathers of the Barnabite Order, containing an explanation of the Gospels for every Sunday and principal festivals throughout the year, had been printed in a large volume. The Homilies being written in a very pure and correct language, the work must be of great help to all mission-

Rev. G. D'Cruz.

Books printed for the Mission.

aries, and particularly to those who are studying the Burmese language. The Life of St. Francies Xavier, the Life of our Saviour in verses, an abridged history of the Old Testament, a Collection of Hymns and Canticles, and other books have been successively published in Burmese. We may say that the Mission is well provided with books both for the vernacular Schools and also for the use of the Native Christians.

Moreover, a fine Church has been erected in a large compound of the School. It is built with bricks, and roofed with tiles. From the entrance into the compound, the front part of the building exhibits a fine and elegant appearance. It has been erected from the proceeds of a subscription. and chiefly from the generous and liberal aid afforded by the two principal Christians of the place, Messrs W. Thisella and M. Cajetano D'Attaides. The latter, in particular has displayed, in the promotion of this good work, a generosity worthy of the olden times of Portuguese ascendancy in India. The Press building has been likewise considerably enlarged. A substantial *zeat* has been erected for the benefit of the Christians, who living at a distance from the town, want a place of rest, where they can stay during the Sunday, and other days, when they have to come to town.

Girls' School.

A very large plank built edifice has been erected for a Girls School. It is intended for an English day-school, and a sort of orphanage and Burmese school, for the daughters of the Karen Christians, inhabiting villages spread about the town. Two native Nuns have been sent from Rangoon, for conducting the Burmese School, and managing the children of the Orphanage. Under God's blessing, it is to be hoped that the Institution will prove productive of much good for the benefit of the Karen population.

In St. Peter's Institution, Karen boys are not only trained up to the studies they have come to master, but they are taught several handicraft professions which in time, will prove of great use to them. Two of the boys understand well photography. Several are good hands in working on wood and metal, as carpenters and blacksmiths.

It is now time to visit the three principal Karen Stations which are situated between the towns of Donabew and Mianaung. In ascending the river as far as Donabew, the first of the three principal Christian stations, that is met with, is that of Mayoka now called Maryland, situated somewhat inland, about seven or eight miles, north of the the above named city, and about three miles distant from the bank of the river. It was in 1864, that the Rev. J. B. Tardivel, a man full of faith and of the spirit of God, resolved to come and settle in a lonely place on the bank of a small creek called Mayoka. The whole country was almost uninhabited. It was covered with tall and thick elephant grass. Since the revolt of a Burmese chief, named Myathun, after the war of 1852 Though overgrown with grass, the land is eminently fitted for the cultivation of paddy. The valiant labourer of Christ said to himself: "I will go and settle in that wild place, with a catechist, and will patiently wait until God will send me some families willing to hear the word of Salvation.

Mayoka or Maryland.

His hope was not confounded. He was living in a bamboo hut. Four or five families came at first to dwell around his hut. In the following year 1865, he erected a large wooden building, which showed the people that the Priest was dertermined to remain among them. The years 1866 and 1867 as well as the following, saw the number of Christians considerably and steadily increasing.

Plank Church.

In 1870, the wooden Church on one hand was too small for the increasing number of converts. On the other, being made of common jungle wood, it was already, after a few years, giving evident signs of approaching decay, in several parts. The Rev. Father resolved to build a new Church of substantial materials, which would not require constant repairing. He selected a spot at a small distance from the one he presently occupied, and began to make bricks. The masonry work was begun and carried on with the utmost activity. The writer has seen the admirable zeal, with which the people, young and old, men and women bore up the fatigue, heat, thirst and sometimes hunger in

Fine brick Church and House at Mayoka.

carrying on the work. In 1872, the building was so far advanced, that it could be comfortably inhabited. Every succeeding year has witnessed fresh improvements. At last in 1876 the Church and the residence of the Priests have been completed. They present a palatial appearance, in the midst of a wilderness.

Two Schools for Boys and Girls.

In addition to this, the Priest has not forgotten the Schools. There are two substantial buildings erected for the two Schools. One of them, the one destined to the girls is made of bricks. Few missionaries would have the physical strength and moral energy to go through a similar amount of labour which appears almost above the forces of human nature. The food on which he supported himself was of the coarsest discription, hardly better than that of a poor Karen. The number of Christians belonging to the place of Maryland, is about 800. During the period under review, a Native Priest, Rev. Pakin, remained with father. Tardivel for about 18 months, when he was sent to the upper country. He was then succeeded by another Priest, the Rev. Moses, who stayed there three or four years. He exchanged his place with the Deacon Carolus, who is now assistant to father Tardivel, and has been ordained priest.

It is to be observed and carefully noted that the Rev. Tardivel has erected those various edifices, without receiving hardly anything from the mission, in the shape of money; nay, he has often refused it, when freely offered to him by the Head of the Mission. He has boldly trusted in Providence and in the aid of his poor christians. With these two resources, he has been able to bring to a successful issue several works which would have appeared impossible of execution in a country or district so destitute of all resources, to a man even who would have had at his disposal a well filled purse. No where has the writer witnessed such an example or instance of perfect confidence in God, so manifestly and abundantly rewarded. It is impossible not to see the finger of God in all that has been accomplished. We must however, not forget nor lose sight of the great fact, that a man, having one object in view, and prosecuting it with unflinching patience and unswerving will, can accomplish great things with small means. It was faith alone, which communicated to father Tardivel, that indomitable courage and firmness of purpose which have formed the very essence of his missionary spirit. God also has been pleased, in several occasions to reward the humble, but strong faith of his servant by allowing, on several trying circumstances, a special interference of his divine Providence, in a manner, if not miraculous, at least, quite extraordinary.

Thinganaing.

North of Maryland, about 8 miles South West of Henzada, in a place called Thinganaing, there is the second Christian Station of importance on the western bank of the Irrawaddy. It is the first that has been established in these parts by the zeal of Catholic Missionaries. Rev. R. Naude, having left Bassein in March 1858, under the guidance of an old Karen, whom he had delivered from the Bassein Jail, directed his steps, at first to a place called Kyinpho, about six miles North of Henzada. No sooner had he arrived at that place, than he found that his guide had imposed on his credulity. After a stay of two months, he saw that the position of the locality, was a very unfavourable one; he left it, and came to settle in another locality called Thinganaing the situation of which has been already alluded to.

Beginning at Thinganaing.

On that spot, there is a small Mango tree grove. There the energetic Missionary, with the help of two Boys he had with him, erected a miserable bamboo hut, the imperfectly thatched roof of which, hardly preserved him from the rain.

He began to have some success among the families living in his neighbourhood. They as well as the pagans joined their efforts, and began to erect with the jungle wood of the forests, a large house 150 feet in length and 30 in width, intended the best part for a Church, and the other part for the residence of the Priest. It was a very commodious place. But being built with common wood, it began soon to give unmistakeable signs of rapid decay in 1869. It was during that period of time, that the work of conversion went on with great energy. Every year the flock rapidly increased, and the good father had the consolation to see himself at the head of a congregation of converts, numbering more than

1000 souls. In 1861 Rev. father Tardivel went to assist the Missionary of Thinganaing. He remained there until the year 1864. Rev. J. Bringaud, was sent to relieve Father Tardivel. He remained in that locality during nearly three years. Deacon Carolus went subsequently to assist Father Naude. Having been afterwards removed to Mayoka or Maryland, his place was occupied by Rev. Moses.

New brick Church and house at Thinganaing.

Father Naude, perceiving the decay that was gradually encroaching on the building that had cost him so much labour and fatigue, though it had hardly stood 10 or 11 years, resolved to erect a new one, made of more durable and lasting materials. The expense he knew would be great, but he trusted in God and the liberality of his Christians. Moreover, he gathered some money from the principal officials of Henzada, and with what he had been able to amass, he resolutely set at work. The work was begun in March 1869. Having contrived to throw hastily a temporary roof on the pillars, he went to occupy it a few months afterwards. The edifice was far from being completed. During two successive years, he laboured hard to have some parts of it gradually finished, until it was at last brought to the present state of completeness. The dwelling place for the priest is connected with the Church. The whole building is a very substantial one, and presents a fine appearance. It is, for the wilds, where it stands, a real monument. It was in 1871, that the energetic Father Naude wished to have a steeple erected in front of the Church. With him, to will and to set at work, is one and same thing. An old undermined dike of bricks, thrown across a stream close to his place, many years ago, by a well-to-do Burman, supplied a good quantity of bricks for carrying on the undertaking. Men and women, who had not the means to give money, contributed to the good work by their labour. The writer has been astonished and, at the same time, much edified in witnessing the zeal and devotedness, the cheerfulness and alacrity displayed by all in furthering the work, every one acccording to his strength and ability. They were all busy like ants. It took two years before the steeple was completed, Two small bells by their merry peals give some life, three times a day, to these silent places, and by their united sound announce, on Saturday evening, that the following day is the day of the Lord, and the day of rest. On Sunday, they are summoning the faithful to gather into the house of their common Father, and offer to him their prayers and supplications, petitions and thanksgiving.

When Father Naude, made his appearance in that district, there had never been there a single Christian or European Priest. It required a great courage and resolution to come alone, attended with 2 boys only, and pitch his tent in the midst of Karen huts, in a district which, in those days, was in great part, covered with jungle. The people, at first, were very shy of him, but, as he could speak their language, they soon readily approached him, and became familiarized with him. As they were often vexed by the Burmans of the neighbouring places, they were quick enough in perceiving that by having an European Priest, they would possess a protector in whom they could trust, and who would be able to defend them from the vexations they had so often experienced at the hand of the Burmans. On this point, they have not been disappointed in their expectation. Father Naude, has been their staunch friend. In fact, he has placed his people in a position not to fear the Burmans. The latter are but too glad to treat the Christians as their equals and their friends. When they have some difficulties, either at Henzada or somewhere else, they call themselves, the disciples of the Priest, and use his name as a means of protection against their opponents. It must be admitted that in all other stations, where a Missionary has established himself, the same instinct of self-preservation has acted in a similar manner. Human considerations have, at first, influenced the Karens in approaching the Priest and placing themselves under his guidance and control. They have obeyed to motives of self-interest, in the beginning; in fact, things could not happen in a way different from this, unless we are prepared to maintain that the grace from above has worked in a miraculous manner, upon the mind of those children of the forests. Providence, doubtless, has prepared the way to the advent of the Missionary in such or such place, and disposed the people to receive him and harbour him among them.

But, as regards the acceptance of the religious instruction by every individual, another element, was absolutely necessary in order to procure conversions. That element was no other but the free and active co-operation of every individual in sincerely and effectually adhering to the truths expounded by the messengers of God, in the Name of Him who had sent them. But this element could only show itself at the time that religion was preached and its truths expounded and brought within the reach of their intellect. It is, but at that moment, that,what is called conversion, can really take place. These few words are written down for the express purpose of anticipating remarks made by persons, who carried by an unenlightened zeal and lacking reflexion, are prepared to condemn every Missionary effort that has the least appearance of human agency, losing sight that the Messenger of Christ, has to deal with men first, and with men, who are gifted with liberty and free will and yield partly to human motives and self interest in the beginning of their conversion.

During the first year of his stay at Thinganaing, Father Naude obtained with much exertion and labour, about one hundred converts. The number rapidly increased, when they were truly convinced that he seriously meant to dwell among them for good. They believed in his earnestness, when they saw him exerting himself to the utmost and straining every nerve, in erecting a good and substantial wood building. From that moment, the people became earnest in attending to the instructions and disposing themselves for baptism. The number of applicants was often so great that the assistants of the Priest, were not able to suffice to the work. The *élan* or impulse thus given, lasted for a few years; then came the most difficult part to be acccomplished viz. completing the summary instructions at first given, and christianizing the thoughts, the affections, the feelings, the ways and manners of the new converts. *Hoc opus, hic labor.* No one, but he who has been devoted to the work of converting Pagans to Christian religion, can understand the amount of patient labour that is required. Schools are the principal means at the disposal of the Missionary, in order to educate well, children of both sexes who will subsequently form the next generation.

Father Naude, with some assistance he received from Government, built two fine Schools, one for boys and ancther for girls. They are situated within the Church's compound. The number of children attending the Schools, has never been considerable, owing to the great distance children are living from the centre of the Church's locality. Perhaps, also, sufficient efforts have not been made in order to have a larger boarding place for a considerable number of children.

Two Schools built at Thinganaing.

In his compound, Father Naude, has also planted a good number of teak trees, which are growing up to a good size and promise to thrive well. They will however yield an inferior quality of timber, which can never bear any comparison with that yielded by trees growing on elevated ground. For the last 4 or 5 years, Father Naude has been assisted by the Rev. Moses, a most zealous and worthy native Priest.

Rev. Father Bringaud, after a stay of three years at Thinganaing directed his steps in November 1867, to a place about four miles west of the large village of Oukpho. He was invited to proceed thither by some Karens, who had relatives in the village of Thinganaing, and likewise by a few Kyens, dwelling in that locality. As regards its situation, the place that has received the appellation, of Mittagon, is a well selected one. It is in the centre of a vast plain, close to the Oukpho Stream, which from Oukpho is lined with villages embosomed in groves of fruit trees. The Oukpho small river issues from the Arracan chain of hills, and discharges its waters in the Irrawaddy, close of the village of Thambradaing. Boats can float on it during almost the whole year, with the exception of about two months. The whole plain is studded with villages. The small ones are inhabited chiefly by Karens, and those of a larger description, by Burmese. There are a few Kyens families dispersed in various localities.

Mittagon Oukpho.

When Father Bringaud arrived, he received from Government,

an extensive piece of land, on which he erected, at first, a modest temporary bamboo building, which was used as a Chapel and a house for his residence. In the following year, in 1868, having gathered a good quantity of teak timber he built the present Church. It is a roomy and strong edifice calculated to last for many years. At the back of the building there are three rooms that afford a sufficient place of residence. In the year 1869, he erected another building in teak also, intended for a Boys' School. It is in every respect, well disposed for the intended purpose. Near it, are the out-offices. The School compound is surrounded with a good paling. The energetic Missionary was not satisfied with what was already done. He wished to have also a good School for the Karen Girls. By his admirable tact, he knew how to obtain pieces of teak gratuitously from Government, and from a Rangoon Firm that was working teak forests in the neighbouring localities. Moreover, by his insinuating manners, he obtained assistance from different parties, who admiring his great zeal and devotedness, were glad to come forward with money to his help. The Girls School is a fine teak building with two stories and a substantial tile roof. There is abundant room for the accommodation of the two Mistresses, and a number of girls who are boarders on account of the great distance that separates them from the villages where their parents are residing. This state of things entails a considerable expense on the Priest, who has to provide food for so many pupils. It is true, parents make occasional donations of rice which forms the staple of food to the people of these parts. The School is managed by two Native Sisters of St. Francis Xavier, who seem to have the qualifications necessary for carrying out satisfactorily the work entrusted to their care. The building was begun in 1874. The compound is enclosed with a good enclosure which separates effectually the Institution from all other places. It is likewise stocked with many fruit trees, chiefly mango and tamarind trees, as well as plantains. The children have a spot of ground where they cultivate flowers and few European vegetables.

Boys School.

Girls' School.

Sisters of St. Francis Xavier.

The whole compound of the Mission contains, at least, seven acres of land. The whole has been given by Government. It was a completely waste spot, when Father Bringaud came to pitch his tent upon it. Now it is a handsome ground planted out with fruit trees, studded with three principal buildings, the Church with its pair of towers and the two Schools. The whole ground is surrounded with a good paling made of teak slabs.

The work of evangelizing the natives has been somewhat slow and gradual; but it appears to have been steady and persevering. No extraordinary occurrence has taken place to bring about a sudden rush of Pagans coming to declare themselves disciples of the Missionary. All has been done, as it ought to be, through the agency of native converts. Father Bringaud has known how to select two good Catechists, one a young man, and another an old one. Both have been men of an exemplary life, at the same time, full of zeal for the conversion of the Natives. Rarely have I seen men of such an extraordinary activity and ardent love for the dissemination of Christian tenets. The number of converts is yearly increasing, by dint of persevering zeal, and prodigious efforts. Christians are to be found in several villages spread at a great distance. In each village, a headman is established for the object of chiefly on Sunday prayer presiding the meeting and conveying instruction to the Christians of the place. They are reminded of the importance of labouring for the conversion of their parents and relatives, living in the same villages or its neighbourhood. The number of Christians in that station, is not less than 1,200.

Building for the Priest's Residence.

Hitherto the Priest was living in a couple of rooms connected with the Church. The accommodation was narrow and insufficient, but the Missionary has put up cheerfully with that inconvenience, until he could manage to erect a building for himself. When the writer visited the station of Mittagon, he was much pleased to see raised up the frame of a good and large house for the accommodation of the Clergy of that Station. I am sure that in less than four months from that date the building shall be completed. It is intended for a double story. It will be the best building that the Mission possesses in the districts. That of the Missionary at Kanotzogon, might be compared with it; but it is not so broad nor so roomy.

The station of Mittagon is lying about half way betweenHen zadah and Myanoung, and in a close vicinity to the river of Oukpho. It possesses many advantages, which are of a great importance. It is also situated at a convenient distance from the chain of mountains called the Arracan Yoma range. The place is as healthy as any one I have seen in lower Burma. The soil is moderately fertile ; but the vicinity of the hills enables men of active habits, to go thither in search of many things from the sale of which they can realize a good profit. Rev. Bringaud is now

Rev. Rouyer.

assisted by Rev. Rouyer, who arrived from Europe in 1877, and the deacon Daniel. The field is a very promising one, and it is to be hoped that with the zeal that animates most of the New Converts, faith will be spread rapidly throughout the district of which Mittagon may be considered as the centre. The Baptist Missionaries, who live in those parts, do all that they can, in order to spoil the work of the Catholic Priest. But their efforts have hitherto entirely failed, nay many of their followers are much inclined to abandon their parts and declare themselves disciples of the Priest.

Prome.

In ascending the river Irrawaddy we meet the important town of Prome, situated on the left or eastern bank, on a sort of Peninsula made by a bend of the river. When the Burmese rule prevailed in Pegu, Prome was the second town of importance in the whole extent of the southern part of the Kingdom. It does not appear that there have ever been Missionaries stationed in that locality. No vestige of Church is ever to be seen. When the English in 1852 occupied Prome, the place was found so unhealthy that the frontiers garrison was removed about 40 miles higher up, to a place called Thayetmyo.

Prome Church.

In 1877, a rail road was opened from Rangoon to Prome, which was the actual terminus of the line. In view of what was soon to come to pass, the Superior of the Mission, has resolved to establish at Prome, a small

Catholic Station for the benefit of the Catholics living there or in the neighbourhood. A small piece of land was obtained from the Municipality, and in the same year an agreement was made with a Burmese Carpenter of Thayetmyo, to build a Chapel, with two rooms adjacent as a place of residence for the Clergyman, who would occasionally visit the place either from Thonzeh, or from Thayetmyo. The building is near being finished. When, however, one has to deal with a Burman, it is impossible to say when the work shall be completed. It is preferable to give a work to a Chinese Carpenter, though his charges would be somewhat high, than to trust it into the hands of a Burman, who will do the work very unsatisfactorily and with delay added over delay. It is a great satisfaction to a Catholic soul, to see that, at last, a place of worship is erected to the glory of God, in a town that has witnessed none but idolatrous temples.

Thayetmyo.

Forty miles above Prome, on the right bank of the Irrawaddy is the town of Thayet with the garrison quartered in fine teak wood built barracks on an elevated and undulating ground. When the English occupied Prome in 1852, they selected it as a place, that appeared in every respect, fitted for such a purpose. But, to the great dissappointment of the military Authorities, the spot proved so unhealthy that it had to be abandoned and the present site was selected by a Commission sent purposely to look out for the most eligible spot for establishing a military cantonment. When the writer visited, for the first time, the town of Thayetmyo in 1856, there was a good wooden church on the bank of the river, near the artillery barracks. On the following year, the Authorities resolved to erect a fort, and as the Church was found to be in a dangerous proximity of the powder Magazine, an order was issued that the Church was to be pulled down, and the sum of Rupees 7,000 was sanctioned for rebuilding a new one. As the old Church had been erected by private subscriptions, it could not be considered as Government property. A liberal donation of 1,700 Rupees was made by Government as compensation and also for removing the materials.

Removal of the Plank Church to Rangoon.

At that time, we had but a miserable place of worship at Rangoon in St John's compound. The Rev. P. Barbe, was sent by the writer, to Thayetmyo, with order to take carefully down all the parts of the building, to place the whole on two rafts and bring them to Rangoon. The work was done which so much care and attention, that not a single plank was broken nor a pane of glass put out of its place. The Church was rebuilt in Rangoon and long used for divine service. The sum of Rupees 1,700 had been sufficient to defray the expense of taking down the building, floating it to Rangoon and setting it up.

Building of a new Church.

With the sum of Rupees 7,000 allowed by Government, Father Pacchiotte, built the present Church on a good piece of ground allotted to him for that purpose. The building was completed at the beginning of the year 1858. Three rooms and a hall connected with the Church afford a tolerably good residence to the Priest. The building having been declared Government property, is kept up, and repaired at the expense of the State. On account of ill health Rev. C. Pacchiotti was compelled to return to Italy. His place was taken by the Rev. Father Guerin, who remained there for three or four years, when he was sent to occupy the important situation of Moulmein.

Father Guerin.

Father Navech.

Father Navech had been sent from Paris to be one of the Directors of the General College, which the Society possesses at Pinang. But, on account of ill health, he was permitted to join the Burmese Mission, where he could find occupations more in harmony with his physical constitution, than the sedentary life of a College could possibly be. He arrived here in the year 1864.

Father Guerin, having been called to take charge of the Moulmein Mission, in the place of Father Ducotey the latter went to take temporarely charge of Thayetmyo, as Father Navech was not yet ready to start up for that place. Father Ducotey remained about six months in Thayetmyo. Father Navech started then for that locality though with an enfeebled health, and somewhat imperfect knowledge of English, he exhibited during the few years he remained at Thayetmyo, the sterling qualities of a good and zealous pastor, and by his simple and mortified habits, he knew to win the respect and admiration of both Catholics and Protestants. The awful scourge, cholera, showed itself in the Thayetmyo Station with great virulence in the year 1870. The good Priest expended all his strength in visiting, day and night, all the patients, both Catholics and Protestants. When the Plague had all but disappeared, Father Navech experienced a slight attack, which was more than sufficient to carry him off. The Doctor, who attended on him, told the writer that Father Navech succumbed to an attack of Cholera, which a child could have easily resisted, but which proved too much for a man who retained hardly more than a spark of life in him. After his demise, the officers to testify their regard for the departed Father, erected, at their joint expense, a fine Monument over his grave, with a suitable inscription.

Father Beart.

In the same year, Father Beart was sent to assume spiritual charge of Thayetmyo in the place of the worthy defunct above named. By the exertions of good Father Navech, a reading club had been begun for the benefit of Catholic soldiers and civilians. There was also a place of amusement. Tea and coffee were served out to those who wished for those beverages. His successer endeavoured to give more extension to the good work. About the end of the year 1872, Rev. H. Beart, was desired to come to Rangoon, and take the place of Rev. A. Bourdon, now promoted to the dignity of Bishop of Dardania, *in partibus Infidelium* and Vicar apostolic of Upper Burma.

The Rev. L. Petit, who had arrived from France at the beginning of 1872, was sent to occupy the station of Thayetmyo. He worked zealously during the five years he stayed at Thayetmyo. The Church was much improved in every way. The building was consolidated, a new floor replaced the old and worn out one, new sacred vessels were imported from Europe, decorations were profusely spread. A good choir was with much trouble inaugurated and the ceremonies were performed as well as it could be in such an out of the way place. Moreover a School was set up for the benefit of Malabar boys and girls. In the year 1877, the Rev. gentleman after having given much trouble to the Head of the Mission, by his inconsistent and imprudent behaviour, left the station.

He was succeeded by the Rev. Father Guerin, who arrived at that place in the very beginning of the year 1878.

Boys' School at Moulmein.

The Rev. Father Zahm, who was in charge of the Church of Mayangon, was appointed to take care of the Church of St. Patrick. He was no sooner in his new appointment, than he exerted himself to the utmost of his abilities to carry into execution the plan of building a new School for the Boys. The necessity of such an undertaking had been duly felt and appreciated by his predecessor who had even begun to collect some funds for that purpose. Father Zahm, who has a special talent for designing buildings and understanding the practice as well as the theory of wooden and brick constructions, resolutely set to work and in the short period of 15 or 18 months, erected the beautiful and vast building, which serves for the Boys who attend the school, and for the Brothers who have the management of it. The cost of the building has been 24,000 Rupees. The greatest part of that large sum has been gathered from various sources, by the industry of the indefatigable Pastor of St. Patrick's.

Not content with what had been just brought to an end, Father Zahm, set his mind upon consolidating the upper part of St. Joseph's Convent, raising its roof, and widening the Verandahs. The work was carried out, in 1877, in an incredibly short space of time, and in a manner that reflects the highest credit on him who planned the repairs and caused them to be executed. The building has been both beautified, and considerably enlarged.

New Chapel at Amherst.

During the year 1878, the people who form the small Congregation of Amherst, seeing that their Chapel had fallen in a somewhat dilapidated state, subscribed among themselves the sum necessary for building a new one larger and better than the former one.

Tamil School at Mayangon.

At Maulmain, in the quarter of the town that is called Mayangon, there already existed an anglo-vernacular School for the benefit of small children of both sexes,- who could not attend the Schools of the Brothers and Sisters in the principal Parish. But in the year 1878, Rev. L. Biet established a school in the Church's compound, for the benefit of the children of the Tamil speaking population. At the same time, he laboured for establishing the centre of a Tamil Congregation in the same locality. By means of a catechist, who visits the members of the Congregation spread all over the town and the neighbourhood, the people are attracted to his place, and are delighted to be able to converse with him, in their own language. At last, after many years of anxious expectation, the head of the mission has had the happiness to see that a serious and earnest effort is being made for establishing a Tamil Mission in Maulmain. It is to be hoped that the work shall, hereafter, receive a greater and ampler development.

Improvements in the Mergui Church.

In the town of Mergui, Rev. Father Cherbonnier, has done much for improving and beautifying the small church of that place. He has had it well furnished with comfortable seats for the Congregation. The additional painting has made it appear very pretty. He has in the year 1877, added in front of it, facing the street a very neat belfry.

Two handsome little bells have been procured from France ; and hoisted up the graceful wooden fabric. They make the air resound with their merry peals. Their united and well accorded tunes is much admired by the inhabitants of the small town of Mergui. It is to the pious liberality of Mr. Georges de Castro, that the Community is indebted for this new improvement. He has been the munificent benefactor of the Mergui Mission during a period of more than sixty years, and has fully entitled himself to the grateful remembrance of the past and present generations of the Christians dwelling in this locality. During 45 years the writer has witnessed the numberless acts of liberality and generosity, towards the support and development of Christianity in Mergui. God seems to have shown how much He approved of his charitable dispositions, by bestowing on him, as he did on the patriarchs of old, an honoured long life, a numerous posterity spread and scattered all over the Tenasserim coast, a respected name and character, enjoying the sincere esteem and well merited respect of all that have known him. On this side of the Cape of Good-Hope, the writer has never come in contact with a more sincere, humble, generous and charitable disciple of Christ. It is truely delightful to meet with such a true and practical Christian, who loved his family, carefully educated his children, faithfully served Government and knew how to use for the service of God and the relief of the poor, a considerable portion of his honestly earned fortune.

Chapel at Henzada.

On another place of this mission, a great desideratum has at last been filled. I allude to the town of Henzada which up to the year 1879 had been without a Church or even a small and humble dwelling for the various Missionaries, who from their principal centres, resort frequently to that station. The head of the Mission, for a long time, had thought of purchasing a small piece of ground, in a suitable quarter, where a Chapel could be erected and an accommodation for the momentary residence of Missionaries passing through that place, could be provided. A favourable opportunity having offered itself, the writer eagerly availed himself of it. He purchased a small piece of land, a little more than an acre, surrounded with a bamboo fence, situated in a most quiet and secluded locality. A Church was erected with teak-wood materials. A spacious room was managed for the accommodation of the priest who visits this place. Moreover, out-offices were erected as well as a house for the residence of the guardian of the place. A sum of Rs. 4,300 was expended towards purchasing the ground and building the Church and the out-offices. Henzada becomes an important place owing to its having become the head-quarter of the Commissioner of the Irrawaddy division.

House at Thonzai.

In 1880, soon after his return from India where he had been compelled to go for the benefit of his health, Rev. Gandon, set at work with the utmost energy for building a good and substantial house in the locality of Thongzai, intended to replace a poor, low and miserable hut-like structure that had hitherto afforded a poor shelter to the priest in charge of the stations. The lower part of the new house affords a sufficient room for the school. In the upper floor, a broad verandah with the portico, is used for a chapel, until the Church shall have been built The auspicious event shall, it is to be hoped, is soon to take place. The station of Thongzai is admirably well situated for Missionary operations, either among the Burmese or the Karens. The Mission's compound is broad and extensive, and may hereafter prove very useful for future purposes.

Church at Letpan.

In the same year, the priest Thomas established in a place called Letpan, at a small distance from Rangoon, on the Dalla side, a fine large and extensive building which he has converted into a beautiful church, reserving for the Priest's dwelling and a vestry, two rooms. As the church is raised nearly ten feet above the ground, the place vacant below is divided into three parts, one large room at each extremity, and a vacant space in the middle, where people can assemble, and shelter themselves from the sun and the rain, before or after divine-service. The building is by far the best finished of all those established in the country, among the Karens. The industry and perseverance of the Rev. Thomas has been displayed by his having converted what was before a paddy field, into a well laid and extensive compound. A large tank has been excavated for securing a supply of fresh water during the dry season. The earth taken from the excavation has been used for raising the ground and placing it above the reach of the water during the rainy season. The poor Priest has much laboured and toiled for completing the work he has so energetically undertaken. The chapel was solemnly blessed among a great concourse of people, by the head of the Mission, attended with the three Priests of the town, and Rev. S. Schmitt. It was in the month of April 1881, that the ceremony was performed. No doubt the Burmese and Karens of the neighbourhood had never witnessed any thing like it. A great dinner was offered to all comers. It is supposed that more than a thousand people partook of the good things prepared for them by the means of a subscription made before hand, only among the

Christians. Mr. J. B. Pereira, of Rangoon, has, by his liberality in helping Father Thomas, entitled himself to the honorific title of Kiaung Taga and to the sincere thanks of the Mission.

Rev. D. Tarolly leaves Thaboo.

During many years, the Rev. S. Schmitt, has been laboring among the Karen population dwelling south of a line drawn from Rangoon, extending in a Western direction as far as that branch of the Irrawaddy called China Bukeer. The first place where a house has been erected, is Shaboa. This small station was begun at first by Rev. D. Tarolly. But the good priest having been attacked and wounded by robbers during the night, he became justly alarmed and leaving Shaboa came to fix himself in a place called Giaung wine, on the Dallah side close to Rangoon. After a stay of a few years in this locality, Rev. Tarolly went to Myaungmia, which had been the first seat of his labors among the Karens. Rev. S. Schmitt, succeeded Father D. Tarolly, at Shaboa. He rapidly enlarged the field of his labors in the neighbouring villages, where he established small chapels which served for the twofold purposes of worship for the small congregations, and of a residence for the Priest, when he visited the station. The principal place which he established, is at Thseitgye on the left bank of the China Bukeer river. Not far from it, in a South-East direction, is the village of Bambwaygon. There also, a small chapel has been erected. The above enumerated places, not to mention others, being situated in the midst of extensive paddy fields under water, during the greatest part of the rainy season, the Priest could hardly remain in such localities, without injuring much his health.

Rev. S. Schmitt's doings in Dallah District.

House and Chapel at Kambet.

Rev. Father Schmitt, selected a good place at the entrance of the Burmese village of Kambet. The ground is high, and well watered by a rivulet of fresh water issuing from the neighboring low hill, which ever flows, even during the dry season. Here a good and substantial house has been erected. It is not finished, and it will take a long time as yet before the work be brought to completion.

In the year 1879, and in the beginning of the following year, a good and substantial Chapel has been erected at a place called Taromaraik a dependence of Kanatzogon, by a fervent Christian named Tsablai, who has sacrificed almost all that he possessed, that he might bear the expense he had incurred for carrying to the end his pious undertaking.

New Boys School at Myaungmia.

In the year 1878-79, the zealous Priest of Myaungmia Father Kern assisted by the veteran Missionary Father Domingo, built a very good edifice intended as a school for the boys of the localities that constitute the mission of Myaungmia. The school is intended not only for day-scholars, but also for boarders. Such a step is absolutely required, because most of the children belong to Parents who live in small villages separated from each other, and staying at a great distance from the centre of the station where is the school. Considerable improvement has been made to the Girls School under the management of the native Nuns of St. Francis, who are showing a most praise worthy zeal in laboring among persons of their sex. It is delightful to see nuns who are Natives of the Jungles, born from Karen descent, performing, in the twofold capacity of Religious and of School-mistresses, multifarious fatiguing and important duties, and, in that double capacity, giving generally great satisfaction to those who are in charge of them, and to the Parents of the children.

On the Institute of St. Francis native Nuns.

Since we have had an opportunity of mentioning the native nuns, it is perhaps interesting to know how that small order has come to be established in this mission. In the year 1874, the writer had occasion, to mention to the Superioress of the Convent of the Good Shepherd, Mary of Angels, how we could employ some of our orphan girls as school-mistresses in the various stations where our Missionaries resided and opened schools, for the benefit of the girls of Karen converts. The undertaking of sending young girls from Rangoon to take charge of those schools was beset with many difficulties, which it is unnecessary to relate. We came both to the conclusion that the establishment of a small religious order for native girls that would be willing to enter it, would, under

God's blessing, be the best means to provide for the native schools, a permanent staff of Teachers. Having matured the plan for somewhile, and fully discussed the way to carry it in execution, it was decided that the small Institution should be placed under the protection of St. Francis Xavier, the apostle of the East Indies and its members be styled Sisters of St. Francis. They would be placed under the direction of the Superioress of the Order of the Good Shepherd at Rangoon, subjected however to the control of the Superior of the Mission. A neat dress of black color was devised by the Superioress, to be the peculiar uniform of the new Sisterhood. It was understood that the principal work of the Sisters would be to take charge of the Girls native Schools, in the localities where they would be sent. Moreover they would have to teach prayers and give instruction to the women that would have to be prepared for the reception of baptism, and also they would visit and encourage those of their sex who would happen to be sick. A set of rules was framed to direct them in the spirit of their holy calling. At present the number of the Sisters is fifteen. They have to teach in the Rangoon Orphanage and in three localities, or distinct stations. They are doing much good, inspire the people with respect and confidence and secure the affection of their pupils. If well cared and carefully looked after, those humble daughters of St. Francis are in a position to render great and important services. It has been deemed prudent not to subject them to too many spiritual exercises, that they might have more time to devote to the service of their pupils. From the moment they become novices, and put on the religious habit, they make single vows, which they renew every year at the feast of St. Francis Xavier. They have to go through a four years probation. When this period is over, they wear a silver cross which is the sign of their being promoted to the religious profession.

One reflexion forces itself on the writer's mind, whilst he was sketching out the establishment of the humble order of St. Francis Xavier. Could not an Institution similiar in every respect, be set on foot for keeping up of boys' schools for the benefit of children of the male sex, in the principal localities of the Karen Mission? The attempt could be made, at first, on a small scale ; then developments could be gradually allowed, in proportion to the number of the young men who would be willing to enter the Institute, and devote themselves to the most important work of educating youth. The greatest obstacle to the carrying out of such a plan is not the difficulty of finding young men willing to embrace such a religious mode of life, but in finding a convenient place where they could be properly trained up in a thorough manner to a religious life and to the practice of those virtues, most befitting their position, particularly the love of God, and the love of their duties for the sake of God. They should be broken to the most perfect obedience by the renouncing to self will. Meanwhile, their instruction should be especially cared for and attended to. The more the mind of men is enlightened under the influence of true religion, the better a man is prepared to work with true zeal and perfect disinterestedness. As the order of St. Francis is but an extension of the order of the Sisters of the Good Shepherd, so the new Institution alluded to in the foregoing lines, would be considered as a development of the order of the Brothers of the Christian Schools. When will this idea be strongly taken up and brought into the region of reality!

Benefactors of the Mission.

In an historical sketch of the mission, it is but just and edifying to mention along with their pious and liberal donations, the names of the more generous donors. In 1877, Mrs. Carmichael made over to the Maulmain Orphanage, a house and the piece of land on which it stands south of the St. Patrick's burying ground. But the greatest and most munificent benefactress to the Mission in general, and to Maulmain in particular, is Mrs. Joana Gomez, who by her industrious, and thrifty habits, has contrived to amass large sums of money. She assisted in the erection of the Mayangon Church with a gift of 4,000 rupees. She likewise contributed towards the building of the new Christian Brother's School in St. Patrick's compound. In the beginning of the year 1883, she has, with a most praiseworthy liberality, given a sum of 12,000 Rupees, to be divided among various Churches, Orphanages and Schools, chiefly of Maulmain, Tavoy, Mergui and Rangoon. Her memory shall be remembered by succeeding generations, her donations duly praised, her name shall ever be coupled with the honorific title of *Kiaung Tagama.* The late Mr. Rob. Rogers has left into the hands of the Administrator General, the sum of Rupees 1,000, in behalf of the Church of St. Patrick's Maulmain.

In Rangoon, Mrs. Martina Porter, has left to the Rangoon town Church, a sum of Rs. 1,000. The late Mr. Hernandez, has spent very liberally considerable sums of money, in levelling the burial ground, and surrounding it with a substantial brick wall. The amount spent was at least Rupees, 10,000. The Chapel in the cemetery, was erected at the expense of a good Portuguese man named Ko Jose.

When the writer built the Convent and Orphanage in Fraser Street, he received a liberal assistance of Rupees 6,000 from Kopho Lewis, the son of Domingo Lewis. Never a more timely assistance came to him, as he was temporarily in little difficulties, having to meet the expense for building the Church, and the Orphanage. Moreover his mind was thinking of building a house for the Christian Brothers who were soon to come and establish themselves at Rangoon.

Mr. Advocate John Thompson must be remembered among the benefactors of St. Patrick's Church, Maulmain. He has given many fine Church's Ornaments and decorations. He has likewise afforded generous aid of money to several of our Priests.

At Mergui, about the end of 1882, the old *Kiaungma* Mrs. Isabella-de-Castro, died at the patriarchal age of more than 88 years. Mention is made of her demise on account of having been the worthy wife of the excellent and generous *Kiaungtaga* Mr. George de Castro. In the beginning of the following year, Father Cherbonnier, with great difficulty, recovered from a most dangerous illness. The congregation of that out of the way place, does not increase. It seems that it is rather decreasing, owing to the great number of people, the young particularly, emigrating to Rangoon. During this last 45 years, the writer believes that the population has decreased by at least one third. This decrease is to be attributed solely to the cause that has just been mentioned.

On the list of benefactors must be placed conspicuously the name of Mr. George de Castro. He erected in or about the year 1847 at his sole expense, the Church of Mergui and the Priest's house. Both buildings having been destroyed by fire in December in 1855, the generous donor had both rebuilt at his own expense, on even a better style than before. He was the chief supporter of the Priests of Mergui, and the neighbourhood. He was also assisting the poor Christians in an unostentatious but effective manner. His name shall ever be remembered as one whose name is indissolubly connected with the Mergui Mission.

The eldest son of Mr. George de Castro named Domingo has been a worthy son of his father. He has built at Tavoy a good house for the Priest, and a fine substantial Church. He has supplied it with ornaments and furniture, and during the Priest's absence he performs as much as a layman could do, religious services, morning and evening in the Church.

Arrival of Brothers at Maulmain.

The station of Maulmain has been singularly fortunate in receiving a Brother and some novices who had left Singapore, after the abolishing of the School that was placed under the management of the Christian Brothers, who were replaced by lay teachers. Such an opportune occurrence has enabled the Brothers to give a fresh impulse to the School under their charge. This has happened in the year 1880 .On the other hand the Convent of St. Joseph's has lost two Sisters, in a very short time, Sister Paula, 1881, and Sister Ann, 1882.

In Rangoon, the new Convent, though built on very extensive dimensions, has been found insufficient for containing the ever increasing number of pupils. It was resolved to extend the right wing where are the pupils of the second School by lengthening it to the extent of eighty feet. As estimated, the cost of the work amounted to Rupees 17,000. The half of that sum was generously contributed by the local Government. The work was begun and completed in the same year.

Mission's Houses repaired.

The two houses of the Mission, where the Bishop and Clergy are living, owing to a defective construction of the roof and upper part of the walls, needed urgent and effectual repairs. When they were erected, workmen skilled in their profession, could not be had in those days, 25 years ago. On the other hand, economical means were to be strictly attended to. In a place, however, like Rangoon with a yearly deluge of rain, followed by an excessive drought 4 months duration, buildings that have been standing for 25 years can hardly be expected not to want great and substantial repairs. The repairs were made in the year 1882, to the small house and in the following year, to the large one, at a cost for both, of a sum a little exceeding eight thousand Rupees.

Missions among the Burmese.

A Burmese Mission has been started at Rangoon, by the zealous Missionary, Rev. H. Kromer. Its principal place, or rather its centre is in the western suburb of Rangoon. The spot is low and swampy. The work was begun in 1881. May it, under God's blessing, prosper and develop itself on a grand scale, and belie the unchristian saying of many, *viz.* that the Burmese cannot be converted to Christian religion. Doubtless they offer a stout resistance to the introduction of the Christian religion, but their stubborness, can be overcome by the same grace that changed Paul from an ardent persecutor into a zealous apostle.

New Convent enlarged.

The Convent of the Good Shepherd, at Rangoon, has received, from Angers, at the end of the year 1882, a valuable reinforcement of four Nuns who joyfully and zealously share in the labors of their elder sisters. In December of the same year, Father Bernard, on account of ill health undertook a voyage to upper India in the hope of being benefitted by the change. After an absence of six months, he came back having hardly derived any benefit from the change of place. Father Sadoux, at first, and Father Baert afterwards, officiated during his absence. Father Cardot, returned to Bassein, and Rev. H. Baert, resumed his former position in the Rangoon Church.

In 1882, Rev. Freynet, has begun the erection of a Church at Thongzai. It is a wooden building. The roof and ceiling are put up. The flooring and walling are still wanting. The sickness that has overtaken the Father of that place, and disabled him for several months, has been an obstacle for gathering the timber from which planks and other materials are to be had, for completing the building. It is hoped that during the rainy season, the timber shall be brought from the forests, and placed in the compound of the Church. Subdeacon Andrew has been promoted to the dignity of deacon.

New Boys' School at Thinganaing.

In 1881, the Boys School building being old and in a much dilapidated state, Rev. Father Naude, set at work to have it rebuilt anew, with good and substantial materials. Two chapels have been erected, one at Mindle and the other at Mwegoe, which have become somewhat considerable stations, south west of Thinganaing Many Christian families are living in the two above named localities. The plan for grouping the Karens in or above a common centre, is the best that can be devised for giving consistency to the Karen congregations and rendering comparatively easy, the spiritual administration, and for establishing Schools which would be frequented by children residing about the neighbourhood. The great obstacle to the progress of religion and civilization among the Karens', is the isolation in which they live, and the almost insuperable barrier thrown in the way of the poor missionary, to whom it is impossible to visit effectually the Christians dispersed upon a vast extent of territory, in small groups of one, three or four houses. As man has been made by his Creator to live in society, it is evident that the mode of life, originally adopted and tenaciously adhered to, by most Karens, is a violation of the law under which he has been brought into existence, as a rational being. No means for effectually bettering the position of him who places himself out of the pale of civilization, can avail. The efforts that are made with a most praiseworthy intention, will never be rewarded with a corresponding success. This subject deserves more than an ordinary mention. It ought to receive ampler explanations, which the contracted limits of an historical sketch, cannot possibly admit. The author alludes to this fact, with the hope that it may catch the eyes of some missionaries, who will act up to it, and try to bring about a great and united effort to remedy the evil, and place the Karen Mission on a more satisfactory footing. *Magna est veritas*, and *prævalebit*

Ordination of the Karen Priest J. B. Paboun.

In the year 1882, Father Kern, at Myaungmia, enlarged on a scale comparatively extended, the Girls School directed by two Nuns of St. Francis. The building as it is at present, offers a pleasant aspect and affords ample room for the numerous inmates of the house. In the beginning of the following year, the Deacon John Baptist was promoted to the Priesthood. As he is a pure Karen both by the paternal and material side, the writer has much pleasure in mentioning that he is the first priest of the race. On the day of his ordination, there was a numerous congregation of his countrymen. It was with a great satisfaction that they heard the joyful announcement that God had condescended to select one of their kin and blood, to be elevated to the dignity of Priest.

Oukpho Mission.

In the Oukpho Mission, Father Bringaud, has of late built several Chapels through the many stations of this extensive portion of the vineyard committed to his care. Some of them are erected with substantial materials. In the North of Father Bringaud's mission, nearer to the town of Myanaung, Father Rouyer has established himself three or four years ago. He has built a good Church roofed with zinc and also a good house for the residing Missionary. Unfortunately the want of schools is much felt. We know from experience that without the agency of schools, the Missionary, with the greatest zeal and exertion cannot do much towards promoting the advancement of the good cause.

Finishing of the Thonzai h.

The Church of Thonzai was begun about two years ago. In proportion as Father Freynet, could gather a few materials and small sums of money, he added yearly, something to what had been done previously. It was in 1883 and 1884, that greater efforts being made, he had the satisfaction to seeing the work completed. It was about the middle of October that the Church was blessed and opened to divine service. It is a strong wooden building that promises to last for many years to come. The Catholics of that locality may be proud of possessing such a fine place of worship.

A little while after, the Deacon Andrew was raised to the Priesthood. A great concourse of people came to witness the ceremony. In the crowd, there were several members of his family. We can easily imagine how great was their joy and happiness on this auspicious occasion. The priest is not very remarkable by his talents or capacity, but as he always has been remarkable by the purity of his life, the regularity of his conduct, the writer has thought that owing to his great humility, God would be pleased to make use of him to do some good work for the Mission.

Father Perret's new Station,

In the beginning of the year 1882, Rev. Perret, arrived from France to reinforce the personnel of the Mission. He is from Savoy, with a strong and well built frame of body. He seems cut to undergo the greatest fatigues. He appears to be of a determined dispostion of mind. He has much difficulty in the Talaindat small Congregation. Owing to complicated occurrences, the writer has been morally compelled to abandon that station. Father Sadoux, and Father Perret removed to a fine place North of Talain-dat, on the bank of the Irrawaddy almost opposite to Donabew. Father Perret, has pulled down the Church of Talaindat, and carried the materials to his new place, where he has already obtained a certain number of conversions among the Burmese and the Karens. May the Almighty, help him in his difficult and arduous task he has undertaken !

At the end of the year 1884, two young Missionaries Rev. Lefebvre, and Maigre, left France for this Mission where they arrived in a good of health.

Death of Father D. Tarolly.

It is the painful duty of the writer to have now to record, with feelings of the deepest sorrow, the death of Rev. Domingo Tarolly, a Tyrolese, who departed his life at the Patriarchal age of 84 years. He was sent by the Propaganda to the Burmese Mission, in the year 1829, and reached the place of his destination the following year. He formed as it were, the connecting link between the Barnabite Fathers who during more than a century, had presided worthily over the destinies of the Burmese Mission, from 1720 to 1832, and the Priests of the Propaganda at first, and the Oblats of Turin next. Owing to the very limited number of Priests, labouring in this Mission, the Rev. Tarolly, was sent to the upper country. It is there, in the year 1832, in the village of Monhla, that the last Barnabite expired in his arms. His name was Jose D'Amato, worthy representative of the illustrious religious family he belonged to. From Monhla, Father D. Tarolly, went successively to Rangoon, Maulmain and Bassein. In the first mentioned place, he contrived by his industry and perseverance to cast Burmese types and print a few books in Burmese for the benefit of the mission. The writer likes to mention that it was in the year 1838, or 1839 that he met Father Tarolly, for the first time. It was from Maulmain, that he went to Bassein and became the founder of the Karen Mission in that district. It is incredible how much he labored and suffered at Myaungmia for establishing a Mission. With his own hands, and the aid he received from inexperienced pupils, he erected a large, substantial wooden building that presented a fine appearance, besides a house for the Priest and a School. In the year 1852, the whole was destroyed by the Burmese because of the war that had broken out, between the English and the Burmese Governments. At the same time, he was seized and carried prisoner to Amarapoora, together with Father Gabutti; but he was set at liberty as soon as he reached that place. Peace being concluded between the two nations, the zealous Missionary went back to his dear Myaungmia, and reconstructed the same kind of buildings that he had set up before. Having fallen sick in 1883, he was removed to Bassein, to have the benefit of a good medical attendance; but he expired in that place, about one month after his arrival. He has always been a man remarkable for the purity and innocence of his life, his zeal and his courage. He was, in a word a true Apostle, full of faith and of the Holy Ghost. He has bequeathed to us the bright heirloom of his virtues, as the most valuable inheritance.

Rev. C. Bertrand, Priest.

The fine establishments such as the Church, Boys and Girls Schools, as well as the Priest's residence, set up with so much labour and expense by Father Bertrand, were threatened with a partial destruction by the gradual encroachment of the river on the bank whereupon stood the buildings. At last, in 1883, the poor Missionary had to pull down his own fine and strongly built house, as well as the roomy Boys School house ; and with the materials he rebuilt the two places on a spot more inland and at a greater distance from the bank of the river. May they be safe for the future, from further incroachments!

Movements of the missionaries.

In 1882, Father Baert went to Europe for the benefit of his health, He returned the following year. He was replaced, during his absence, by Rev. A. Cardot, who had to leave the Karen Mission near Bassein where he was beginning to do much good. At the end of the year 1883, Father Gandon having, on his urgent demand, been relieved from the charge of St. Patrick Church, Maulmein, went to Bassein to assist Father D'Cruz, but in particular, to undertake the management of the press, which required an intelligent supervision. He succeeded very well in that employment. Rev. A. Cardot was appointed to succeed him in Maulmein. Soon after his having assumed charge of that station, he made an important improvement in the lower floor of the Convent by raising it six or eight inches and opening drains for the free egress of the water.

In 1883, Father Bringaud requiring a change of climate, went to Europe in March, and returned in October. His health had considerably improved. During his absence, Father Sadoux acted for him at Mittagon.

Success of the School.

It is with pleasure that the writer had to mention the great success obtained by our schools, both in Rangoon and Maulmein. The convent in the first named place, passed in the Middle School Examination eleven candidates out of a total of 13 presented. It is by dint of great exertion from the part of the heads of our Institutions, that such success has been obtained during the year 1883-84.

The writer's voyage to Europe.

Urged on by the repeated entreaties of kind friends, and also feeling the want of rest in the climate of Europe, the writer left Rangoon on the 3rd of May 1884, and on the 6th of June reached Marseille. On the 10th he arrived in London, where he stayed a month. After several trips through England, Holland and France, he returned to the seat of his labors where he arrived on the 25th of October.

During his absence, the demon of discord seems to have worked his utmost, to sow the seed of dissention in the midst of the Tamil Congregation, divided then into two parties. The contest had reached the highest point of acerbity, when the writer arrivea at Rangoon. But thanks to the God of peace, all traces of ill feelings seem to have disappeared. Peace and union are now kniting and cementing the various members of the congregation toge-ther, and linking them to their pastors. The writer wishes to leave it recorded for the benefit of those who will come after him, that the only way to deal with the people when they happen to quarrel on a grand scale, is to listen patiently to what each party has to say, to thank them for the information they afford. Meanwhile, he must speak well of the persons of the opposite party and give them to understand that he has heard persons whom they look upon as enemies, making use of kind expressions towards them After this preliminary disposition, recourse must be had to religious considerations, to be enforced with great earnestness, on the point of forgiving mutual offences. When they appear much excited and red with anger, the pacificator ought to be with a calm and unrufled countenance. Then he must avoid to say a word about the past disputes. Let him leave to time the cure of the moral distemper. Time is a powerful dissolvent, which can dissolve the animosities amassed in the heart and in the mind, cause them to disappear more effectually, than all the reasonings which could be brought forward.

Rev. Bernard's Voyage to India.

In the month of January, 1884 Father Bernard being very ill, went with the writer's permission, to Upper India, in the hope that the cold prevailing in those parts, at that season, might procure a beneficial reaction. He at first felt well, but soon after, he was seized with a dissentery that very nearly proved fatal to his life. He, however, recovered, and returned to Rangoon not much improved in health. He continued to stay in the mission for about

10 months, with a health always declining. At last, he left for Europe in the month of March, 1885. His head appears to have been the seat of his disease. It was much affected. It is to be feared that he will never be able to live in this climate, without being exposed anew to the same infirmities.

Several posset of the Mission.

Mergui has been exceptionally nnfortunate during the latter part of the year 1885, and the following year 1886. It was in the month of December that the patriarch of the Mission, the Kiaung Taga Mr. Georges de Castro died on the patriarchal age of 98 years. During a period of more than 60 or 70 years, he had been truely the pillar of the Mission at Mergui. It was through his exertions that the community of Mergui and also that of Tavoy remained for a long time in a rather flourishing condition, despite the prolonged absence of clergymen. In another place of this small work, a well deserved tribute of praise has been bestowed on him. May he enjoy the splendid reward richly merited by his good works!

Not long after the demise of the worthy Kyaung taga, another great calamity beleif the unfortunate congregation of Mergui. The Rev. Father Cherbonnier anxious to visit a Christian congregations of Karens, living in a village near the kaday river, went in his boat on the 8th of January 1886, for the purpose of reaching early on the morning, the mouth of the small Kaday river. Untill 2 o'clock in the morning he remained at the helm. Seeing that the mouth of the river was close by, he went into his cabin to lay down and sleep. On the dawn, of day, the priest's boy prepared a cup of coffee for his master as he used to do, on such occasion. The boy waited for a while hoping that his master would soon awake. Seeing no movement inside of the cabin, he called the priest, but no answer was given.He opened the door, calling him and pulling him by the leg. No sign whatever of awaking was given. The poor lad was at last convinced that the Priest was really dead. Instead of prosecuting the voyage, the boat-men hastily returned to Mergui with the inanimated remains of their priest. The grief and sherieks that arose from amongst the Christians and even the Pagans can more easily be imagined than described. On the following day, the young amiable priest was interred in the burial ground, by the side of his great friend and supporter the Kiaung taga, Georges de Castro, in the midst of the tears and lamentations of his spiritual children.

In the same year, on the 4th of September, 1886 the Mission received a heavy and fresh blow, by losing, in a most tragical and unexpected manner, another of its good and fervent missionaries. The Rev. Father Biet, had gone to pay a short visit at dusk, to a member of his congregation who was living at a very short distance from his own habitation. While he was drinking a cup of tea with his friend and his family, three assassins rushed into the house and cut down with their knives the Rev. Father's friend Mr. Ramos, for that was his name, who had gone to see what people were coming in. He had hardly strength enough to drag himself at the entrance of the door leading into the hall, when he expired. The ruffians afraid lest the priest would subsequently give evidence against them, fired at him three times with a revolver. He endeavoured to escape by a back door but it was unfortunately found to be barred. Then returning back, he endeavoured to escape by the staircase. It was at that moment that he received three or four stabs with a knife, rolled down the stair-case and was found dead at the bottom. This horrible murder has deprived the Mission of a zealous labourer in the prime of life, and well acquainted with the English, Burmese and Tamil languages which are necessary, to a Priest at that station.

Fortunately Providence seemed to have prepared relief in anticipation for the losses the Mission had met, by sending out in the begining of 1885, two young Priests, Messrs. Lefebvre and Maigre, who joined the Mission in the month of January 1885. Had it not been for this timely arrival, the head of the Mission would have been placed in a most difficult and embarrassing position.

It is in this year also, that Father Guerin, erected a fine house next to the Church in the Rangoon Cantonment. The cost of the building of the house was 5,500 Rupees. The first sum Rs. 5,000 is entirely due to the generous and liberal donation of Rev. Father Guerin. The remaining 500 Rupees were added by the Mission. The house was intended as a comfortable place of residence for the clergyman in charge of the Cantonment Church, and also as a fitting place for accommodating the missionaries in the time of the annual spiritual retreat. We ought also to mention that it was in the midst of the same year 1885, that Rev. Felix Guerin, was appointed Provicar of the Mission. So, the situation left vacant by the final departure of the very Rev. Father Bernard from the Mission, in which he had laboured for so many years, was occupied by the very Rev. Father Guerin in its two fold aspect.

The post of Mergui having become vacant by the death of Rev. Father Cherbonnier, Rev. S. Smith, after having remained during about 16 years among the Karens, living in the West of Rangoon, was transferred to Mergui and Tavoy, on the Tenasserim Coast.

The place occupied by the regretted Rev. Father Biet, was immediately but inadequately filled up. Father Cardot, assisted by a young Priest named de Chirac, did the work required in the two parishes of St. Patrick, and Mayangon. This temporary arrangement has been going on until the month of February 1887, when Father de Chirac, has established himself in the place, occupied by the defunct Louis Biet.

It is with great pleasure and a legitimate pride, that mention is made of the successful efforts made by the Sisters of the Convent of the Good Shepherd, to raise more and more the standard of education of the young ladies committed to their care. In the month of March 1886, they presented four candidates, for admission to the entrance examination of the Calcutta University. Their well meant efforts have been rewarded with a glorious success. Of four candidates presented, three passed. This is the first instance in Burmah, of three young ladies having passed successfully the entrance examination. The news of this unexpected triumph, has made a great impression all over Burma. People from every corner of the land, applauded this unlooked for and hitherto unheard of success.

Father Perret, was at first successfully working among the Burmese. He had already founded a mission in a village called Yebauk, situated in a very fine locality on the left bank of the Irrawaddy, almost opposite to the town of Donabyu, but the rising of Dacoits in every part of the Province terrified the villagers to such an extent, that all dispersed, in every direction and the poor priest with his School Master was left alone to take care of himself in the best way he could. The confusion that ensued compelled the worthy Priest to abandon for a moment the place which he had cultivated with so much zeal and devotedness.

Sketch of the causes of the rising of Dacoits.

Perhaps it is as well to mention here, the several causes that have worked together to produce those various uprisings which like so many small earthquakes have been felt in almost every part of what was called British Burmah. It is surprising to see the population of this part of Burmah, which had enjoyed for more than 30 years the blessings of peace and good Government, should have overlooked them, to show signs of dissatisfaction to Government, bordering on revolt, throughout the whole country, with the exception of the Tennasserim coast. In giving a summary account of what has taken place almost simultaneously in Upper and Lower Burmah, we will see that the same causes have acted throughout the whole country, for producing the results we have witnessed. In November 1885, an English expedition ascended rapidly the river Irrawaddy and reached Mandalay, almost at the same time that the Court was informed that the enemy had left Rangoon. The King and all the inmates of the palace were at once arrested and lodged safely on board of a vessel under a strong guard. A large Burmese military force was then concentrated in the capital and in the neighbouring places. The English remained satisfied with disbanding the men and allowing them to return to their villages and carry away their arms and ammunitions with them. This capital mistake from the part of the English Commissioner, has been the cause of all the robberies, dacoities, and murders that have subsequently taken place. Those men soon spread themselves all over the country. Having no means of existence, since no pay was allowed to them, they betook themselves to all sorts of disorders. They robbed their countrymen without mercy. To this must be added the treachery of many members of the Burmese Government, who under hand excited the rabble of disbanded soldiers to raise the standard of revolt, against the English, in favour of the future monarch of Burma. The Phongyes also instigated by the same officials, made use of a religious pretext to sow the seed of discontent against the conquerors. They were made to believe that their religion was in imminent peril of destruction, since they were deprived of a Burmese King who is held as the essential supporter of Budhism in Burmah.

From Mandalay, as from a focus of discontent, emissaries with proclamations from certain phongyes and also from Burmese officials, were sent down to Lower Burma. In a short time, the people of these parts were thrown at first in a state of ferment, confusion and alarm. They did not know what to do; they hesitated between yielding obedience to their present rulers ; and also the fear lest perhaps a new King of Burmah would arrive and drive the English out of the country. The mass of the people, however, remained faithful to the English Government. But a certain number of idlers, vagabonds, opium-smokers, headed sometimes by Phongyes, sometimes by people sent down from Mandalay, rose in many directions, particularly in the districts of Bassein, Henzadah, Shwaygyin, and Pegu. They did a great deal of mischief not only to Government, but to the unfortunate villagers who, in many instances, seeing themselves violently deprived of their property, had also to witness the conflagration of their dwellings. As regards the mission, the losses have been insignificant except in the district of Okpho where three or four small christian villages have been burnt down. The gangs of robbers crossing over the country, in all directions, have been without thinking of it, the instruments of effecting some good among the Karen rural population. They have felt the necessity of living together and forming large villages. Under the leadership of their Pastors, they have clubbed together, and organised means of resistance, which have effectually protected them against the Dacoits. Though at first, the Karens deserted their dwellings for fear of the Dacoits, they acquired the knowledge that by living together in large villages, they enjoyed an incomparably greater security than they ever experienced when they were living under what I will call a system of isolation.

The statistics also of the year 1887 show to demonstration that the uprising of the so called dacoits has been the cause that a greater number of applicants for baptism, have presented themselves, than they ever appeared in former times.

In the month of August 1885, the Mission met with a new and unexpected trial. The Rev. H. Baert, without a shadow of reasonable motive, without communicating his resolution to any of his Brother Priests, left on a sudden Rangoon and the Mission. Nearly a month had elapsed before news of his whereabouts could be obtained. The first reliable news about him, was obtained through a police officer who came to ask the writer, whether he was aware that a certain Priest, name unknown, was at Padaung, a large village, South of Prome, on the right bank of the Irrawaddy, leading an absolutely idle life. With this information, we could easily guess who the man was. The difficulty was to compel him to leave, what we could call, his hiding place. Owing, to the threats and energetic language of one of our Missionaries, Mr. Baert, thought that it was no longer safe for him to remain at Padaung. He therefore left that place and crossed the mountains that separate the valley of the Irrawaddy from Arakan, and went, after a short stay at Kiaukphiu, to the capital of India, where he has been since living, unknown to any one.

In 1885, considerable additions were made to the Brothers' School in Maulmain. The compound also received a certain extension in the direction of the Priest's house. New out-offices have been erected. The building now is sufficiently roomy and has rather a smart looking appearance. It is amply sufficient for all the requirements of the Institution.

In the year following, Rev. Father Cardot, re-built a new refectory for the benefit of the Sisters of the Convent of Maulmain. It occupies the same place as the old and much dilapidated one which has lasted about 30 years.

St. Paul's New School.

For many years the straitness and narrowness of the locality and buildings of St. Paul's School, Rangoon, were deeply felt, and bitterly deplored by the Head of the Mission and the Director of Public Instruction. But the difficulties staring in the face consisted first in obtaining a suitable piece of ground, and, next to that, a sufficient sum of money for building upon it. It must be here recorded that Brother Valens, the Director of the Institution of the Christian Brothers, had exerted himself much in order to obtain a piece of ground. The best and largest piece he had applied for, was finally and flatly refused Then with his wonted tenacity of purpose he turned his attention to another piece of ground, close to the same one that had been refused. Whilst he was parleying with the authorities, little progress had been made towards securing the land. When the writer returned from Europe, he took the affair in hand, he did not meet with much difficulty in obtaining a large piece of ground, nearly 9 acres in extent. The place had at first a very ugly appearance. It looked in some parts like a marshy swamp ; but it was easy to perceive that the water that covered a small portion of the land, could easily be turned away. With this conviction the application was confidently laid before the Municipality. The Committee after a mature consideration, came to the unanimous decision that the application should be acceded to. The demand was almost immediately granted, with a good grace.

The Deputy Commissioner Captain Adamson, and Mr. Clarke, the Engineer to the Municipality, assisted much the writer in having the transaction settled quickly and satisfactorily. To both of these gentlemen, the writer tenders his heartfelt thanks. This happened in the month of March. In the beginning of April, the trenches for the foundations were opened. The writer felt uneasy about the nature of the ground that was to support the walls of the building. It was a soil formed from the deposit of the water which had formerly covered that spot. Two Engineers were called to come and give their opinion as to the nature of the ground on which the building was to be erected. Their suggestions were eagerly accepted and scrupulously followed. They declared that the ground was perfectly safe. The work went on quietly but vigorously. It was finished and completed within twelve months, and thanks be to God, no accident happened which could endanger the lives or limbs of the workmen. Meanwhile the work of raising the land, on the West and North of the house, and particularly on the East, was carried on with great activity. A sum of more than 3,500 Rupees was expended upon that important improvement. The total expense both for erecting the building and levelling the ground, amounts to the sum of 103,000 Rupees. How has this sum been covered? Where has the money come from, to meet such a tremendous expense? From two sources.

1st from the Municipality of Rangoon which allowed a grant of Rs. 30,000. 2nd, from the sale of the houses and ground which were occupied by St. Paul's School, which realized Rs. 55,000. The total sum netted from these two sources was Rs. 85,000. The difference between the receipt and the expenditure is not less than 18,000 Rupees. This sum has had to be procured by the writer in the best way that he could. From the Fund of the Holy Childhood about 10,000 Rupees have been taken with the full consent of the Director of the work, who told him that the generous allocation in favor of the Mission was considerably raised during three years, in view of the great expense which was to be incurred in erecting St. Paul's School, which shelters a great number of Orphans. A large area for play ground roofed with zinc, has been prepared, disposed and arranged at the sole expense of the Christian Brothers.

Church in Pegu.

In the beginning of the year 1886, the town of Pegu, having become connected by rail with Rangoon, has acquired a great importance. Government have erected, besides the public buildings, a Municipal School, an hospital and a dispensary. Moreover the ground has been drained. What was formerly but a swampy land, has become a well laid out ground. Good looking buildings are springing up in every direction. Some Catholic families having settled thither, the writer much pressed by a good and fervent Christian, Mr. Clancey of the Survey Department, came to the determination of having a chapel erected at Pegu on a piece of ground generously given by Mr. Dias. It is a wooden building that looks well. It has cost about 6,500 Rupees of which the Misssion had to pay 3,500 Rupees. A sum of 2,000 Rupees had been promised at first, but owing to causes which need not to be recorded, the Head of the Mission hes had to pay, much against his will, an additional sum of 1,500 Rupees.

In the month of January 1886, two young Priests, Messrs. J. B. Luce, and Charles de Chirac, arrived from France to reinforce the Mission.

The Boys School at Bassein has not much progressed as regards the studies. It is a purely Burmese School. The deficiency of good Masters, and a want of active and stimulating supervision are the two real causes of the inferiority that has been, oftentimes remarked by the Government Inspectors and by the writer himself, There are, however, two points in which the writer is glad to call the attention of the reader, because they have shed a certain lustre on the Institution, *viz*, the Survey class, in which several boys have learned land measuring, and thereby qualified themselves for obtaining small situations uuder Government. Many boys have already obtained employments which enable them to maintain themselves and their small rising families. Father D'Cruz, has always had in his mind a desire to create a sort of industrial School, in which boys cculd learn some professions which would be subsequently a means of gaining a decent livelihood. The idea in theory is a capital one. But practice shows that our Christian boys, particularly the Eurasians, cannot compete with the natives of Bengal or Madras. The latter work as well as the Eurasians, and at a much lower rate of wages. Moreover, they require hardly more for their support than one third of what will be sufficient for the maintenance of their competitors. There is only one line opened to Eurasians, that of apprentice Engineer. The workshop. set up at Bassein is intended to train up boys in that line of business. Father D'Cruz, began with very limited means at first; but assisted, hereafter, by the advice and the purse of Mr. Murphy, a practical Engineer, he has been able to give a greater development to the works, so much so, that many boys Burmese or Karens, can receive a fair training in that profession, and be enabled, hereafter, to earn their livelihood. Intelligence and perseverance in carrying on this branch of industrial training are the things required to ensure success.

Successes obtained by the Missionaries.

It is truly gratifying to mention the great successes that have been achieved by our Missionaries among the Karen population, during the period under review. It is a subject for great gratitude to divine Providence, for having blessed in a special manner the efforts of the zealous servants of Christ. It is in almost all the districts, that the progress has taken place in a conspicuous manner. But we must acknowledge that it is in the two districts of Bassein and Okpho, that the most wonderful progress has been achieved. The achievement has been accomplished under the most difficult circumstances; intended in appearance, to thwart the growing of the good seed deposited in those parts. The two districts that have been noticed above, as deserving a special prominence, are the parts of the district lying in the North-East of Bassein, and the northern portion of the Okpho Mission. In those two districts the number of converts has been 340 each, altogether 680, for both places. Never in any former period, had the annual return of converts, reached a total above 600 baptisms of adults, which is the number obtained from the 15th August 1885 to the 15th August 1886. The highest number obtained was that of the preceding annual period; it amounted to a little more than 600 But in this year, the number of Baptisms of adylts exceeded 1500.

In the foregoing pages, the writer has alluded to the fact of the political disturbances of the country. He firmly believes that the fear of the Dacoits on oneside; and the hope, on the other side, of finding a protection against their enemies in the person of their spiritual guides, have acted together in shaking off the natural apathy of the Karens, and have induced them to adhere to Christian Religion, which they had already become acquainted with, but had hitherto remained indifferent in embracing. This surmise of the writer has been confirmed by the distinct declarations of many of our missionaries.

Another fruit produced by the appearance of the Dacoits is the following. The Karens have now seen the benefit and advantage of dwelling in villages. Nct long ago, having had the occasion to visit the village of Kanatzogon, the writer was delighted to find there, instead of a few straggling houses built here and there, two villages North and South of the Church. Each had 35 houses at least. The dwelling places were high and roomy, raised upon substantial posts, offering an unsual comfort for the inmates dwelling therein. On the Sunday, that he spent there, he complimented them in the Church, for the great improvement that had taken place in Kanatzogon, and told them that, at last, they had met with his most cherished wishes. He told them they had now given an evident sign of civilization, and that they will not be slow in appreciating the benefit of living in community with their fellowmen.

Blessing of the corner stone of the Church at Myaung Mya.

The zealous priest of Myaung Mya, Revd. Kern had long nourished the idea of erecting at Myaung-Mya Station, a strong, solid brick church to take the place of the old and much worn out wooden building erected by the Revd. Father Domingo in 1855 For a year or two, Revd. Kern had been slowly but perseveringly amassing the materials necessary for building his Church. He had all the bricks made upon the spot ; fresh water sand could be procured without much difficulty. Lime also, through the numberless creeks which intersect the country, could be brought by boats even from a distant place, with little expense. In the beginning of the month of August, the trenches were opened for the foundations and in about a month, the masonry work was brought up one foot six inches above the level of the ground. In his enthusiasm, the zealous pastor would not let pass the opportunity offered to him, of laying down the corner stone of the building, without having it done with a great solemnity. The Head of the Mission, as well as his Provicar, went to Myaung-Mya on the 27th of September. What was their surprise on their arrival at 9 p.m., to find that almost all the Catholic Congregation of Bassein had gathered in Myaung-Mya for that important ceremony. A great crowd of them had come to receive us at the landing place. Instead of a regular band, we had eight or ten Chinese Christians with their tam-tams, making such an unearthly *vacarme*, that they terrified the pariah dogs of the streets to such an extent. as to save us from hearing the horrible howling and barking of those brutes. The house of the Priest was splendidly illuminated. From the top of the verandah, the writer stood for a while admiring the immense crowd that was, wave-like, moving and rolling before him. He addressed them a few words, imparted unto them his blessing, and bade them to return each of them to his place, for it was nearly 10 o'clock at night.

The following day, at 7 o'clock in the morning, the sun shining with a radiant effulgence, enlivened the scene where the ceremony was to be performed. Everything having been done according to the prescriptions of the ritual, an allocution was addressed to the vast congregation that was present. Immediately after having left the ground, we proceeded to an improvised chapel, to celebrate the holy Sacrifice of the Mass. After the Gospel, another allocution was made in Burmese first, and then in English. At a quarter past 9, the ceremony was over.

The Pastor of Myaung-Mya was, and rightly so, overjoyed at the successful inauguration of the beginning of the church.

In company with the Provicar apostolic, the Bishop left Myaung Mya to visit the station of Kanatzogon. We had the satisfaction of finding about 75 persons prepared to receive confirmation. The schools are in excellent order. The only painful object to be seen, is the gradual encroaching of the river on the bank in front of the church.

The writer cannot leave the two places of Myaung-Mya and Kanatzogon without mentioning that several chapels have been erected in these two districts during the last twelve months. Some are very decent little constructions, where the Priest, at the time of his visitation of the place, can find a resting place. On Sundays, the Christians assemble therein to perform their devotions. Revd. Bringaud was telling me that the number of chapels, throughout his extensive district, was above 35. Some of them were becoming and substantial buildings.

The Mission among the Khyiens has not been hitherto productive of extensive results. Let us hope that its humble beginning vill be attended with better and more important results.

During the year 1887 the Mission of Okpho has had a calamitous wind blowing upon it, and blasting for a while, the progress of education ; but it is to be hoped that this misfortune will be succeeded by an era of prosperity.

During the same year, our schools, both in Rangoon and Maulmain. have been successful in passing pupils for the Calcutta University Entrance examination : three from the Rangoon Convent, three from the Rangoon Christian Brothers, and one from the Maulmain Convent.

St. Vincent de Paul's.

It is with a sincere regret and deep sorrow that the writer confesses to a great forgetfulness for not having mentioned the Institution in this Mission of the Society of St. Vincent de Paul. It has been established in this Mission on the 17th of October, 1883. The object of the members of the Brotherhood is to visit the poor at home, imparting therein religious consolations, giving wholesome spiritual advice and affording material aid and relief. They endeavour to reform sinners, bring them back to the path of duty. They stir up the lukewarm to a diligent and fervent Christian life. In a word they do all possible good, both temporal and spiritual. They endeavour to gather alms which their charitable hands will distribute with love and discretion. May God by his blessing, cause the fructification of this Association. !

Revd. Khromer at Nyandoon.

In the beginning of August, Revd. H. Khromer finding the field assigned to him, too narrow, for the ardour of his zeal, has desired to go among the Burmese and Karens to give full vent to his energy and activity. He has selected the large place of Nyandon to settle there, and from that village, he radiates in every direction. chiefly among the Karen population dwelling in the neighbouring villages. He has, it seems, already obtained some success, and there is a fair hope that he will gain a large number of adherents. His health, thanks be to God, appears to remain good.

The Missionaries resolve to celebrate in the following year the golden Jubilee of the Head of the Mission.

In the month of November, last year, when the Missionaries were assembled for their annual retreat, they resolved, before being separated, to celebrate during the course of the ensuing year, the golden Jubilee of the Head of the Mission. They made all the preliminary arrangements concer ing the details of that ceremony. They determined to invite th Bishop of Upper Burma and that of Malesia and also the hea of various Institutions. No other object was contemplated about the ceremony, except to give it a purely religious character. t was intended to be merely *a fête de famille.* But when it became known in town, that the Missionaries had resolved to cele. brate the golden Jubilee of their Superior, in the following year, many gentlemen of Rangoon came forward of their own accord and requested the favor of being allowed to take an active part in the intended proceedings. Foremost among them was the Judicial Commissioner Mr. W. F. Meres. He expressed the earnest wish both in his name and that of his friends, that the ceremony intended to do honour to the Head of the Catholic Mission, should assume a wider range and include members of the various denominations. As the Bishop, he said, had by his labours done good to all, irrespective of creed and nationality and attracted the respect and the consideration of all, it appeared fit to render as much as possible unsectarian the contemplated demonstration.

With these views in his mind, Mr. Meres had two interwiews with the very Revd. Guerin who, in the absence of his confreres', had the entire management of the arrangements to be made for the intended ceremony. The result of these pourparlers, was the convocation of a meeting composed of twenty of the principal European inhabitants of the city, under the presidency of Mr. Meres It was resolved that a subscription should be circulated to raise funds intended to serve as a public recognition of the services of Bishop Bigandet not only in the Missionary field, but also as a scholar and philanthropist. The produce of that subscription was to be employed in the following manner; a sum of money of Rs. 2000 should be presented to the Bishop, and the remaining money should be devoted to form a fund to make an endowment for the advancement of scientific and technical education, in Burma, coupled of course with his name.

The day for celebrating the Jubilee was fixed for the 7th February 1887. All the Missionaries hastened from their respective place to Rangoon. It is with feelings of deep gratitude that is recorded here the generous offer of the Irrawaddy Flotilla Co. to issue tickets for a free passage to all of them, both for coming to Rangoon and returning to their respective stations. A high mass was said in the Catholic Church of St. John the Baptist, in the Cantonment. The place was crowded to overflowing. The sermon was preached by the Right Revd. Bishop Gasnier. The tall figure and splendid flowing beard of the orator, rivetted on his person the eyes of the whole Congregation ; his powerful voice contributed also to secure his hearers' attention, from the commencement of his sermon to its close.

After Mass, there was a large gathering of visitors who came to offer their felicitations to the subject of the feast. All the clergy breakfasted at the Cantonment Parochial House, with the very Revd. Provicar. On a sign from his part, the Revd. Kern rose, came forward and read a beautiful piece of latin verses, composed by him for the occasion. It was admitted at all hands, that it was a composition elegantly written both as regards the style and the beautiful sentiments that were given expression to.

In the afternoon, the writer went to town to receive the several addresses that were to be presented to him. It ought to have been stated that, on the morning of that day, the Sisters of the Good Shepherd had presented their address accompanied with the offering of articles of their own working.

At four o'clock, the Brother Director of St. Paul's High School attended by the several Brothers and followed by a crowd of his pupils, read an address. His pupils read another short one in verses. They then presented a costly diamond-ring, the price of which had been defrayed by their voluntary contributions.

The congregation of the Church of St. John's the Baptist presented an address in Burmese. Though not blessed with wealth, they contrived to raise among themselves a sum of Rs. 600 which was devoted to the purchase of a carriage and pony, which was offered as a mark of respect and affection toward their old Tsayadau. It is not necessary to say that the gift was accepted with the warmest acknowledgments.

The old parishioners of the writer, sent also an address from Penang, as well as the Christian Brothers of that place.

The Tamil Congregation offered also one in their own native language.

At five o'clock, the great public meeting at the Town-Hall took place. Never such a large gathering had been seen in Rangoon on any former public occasion. The meeting was presided by the Judicial Commissioner. All the civil authorities were present on the 'platform.' The chairman having opened the meeting with a few preliminary remarks, called upon the Government Advocate Mr. C. E. Fox to deliver the first speech. Then followed Dr. Marks. Mr. D. M. Gray the Editor of the *Rangoon Gazette* made the concluding speech. When the speeches were over Mr. C. E. Fox was desired by the President to read the address prepared by the General Committee, representing the public of Rangoon. As a matter of course, a reply was made by him to whom the address was directed. The members of the Society of St. Vincent de Paul presented also their congratulatory address.

The meeting was then pronounced dissolved. The Bishop had to receive the warm congratulations of those who could come near him. It ought to be recorded that the celebration of the Jubilee, commenced at the Orphanage at about 2 o'clock. The usual addresses were read in Burmese and a silver cigar case and a snuff-box were presented, with signs of great joy and contentment.

On the following day, the 8th, the Bishop went as usual to say Mass at 6 o'clock in the Convent. In the afternoon, at 3 o'clock the writer went there again, with Bishops Bourdon, and Gasnier, and all the Priests of the Mission. Congratulatory addresses were presented by the children of the first and second school. They offered as a present, a gold-watch with a heavy gold-chain, the amount of which, had been defrayed entirely by the voluntary contributions of the Pupils of the School.

In the evening of that day, at 8 o'clock, the Christian Brothers gave a very successful dramatic entertainment which was attended by a great crowd of people, who appeared delighted with what they saw and heard.

Here we bring to an end the Outline of the History of the Mission. We hope that as years are rolling on, it will be continued.

FINIS.